THE ULTIMATE GUIDE TO SKINNING AND TANNING

Books by Monte Burch

The Ultimate Guide to Calling and Decoying Waterfowl
The Ultimate Guide to Making Outdoor Gear and Accessories
Field Dressing and Butchering Upland Birds, Waterfowl, and Wild Turkeys
Field Dressing and Butchering Rabbits, Squirrels, and Other Small Game
Field Dressing and Butchering Deer
Field Dressing and Butchering Big Game
The Field & Stream All-Terrain-Vehicle Handbook
Denny Brauer's Jig Fishing Secrets
Denny Brauer's Winning Tournament Tactics
Black Bass Basics
Guide to Calling & Rattling Whitetail Bucks
Guide to Successful Turkey Calling
Guide to Calling & Decoying Waterfowl
Guide to Successful Predator Calling
Guide to Making Outdoor Gear and Accessories
Pocket Guide to Seasonal Largemouth Bass Patterns
Pocket Guide to Seasonal Walleye Tactics
Pocket Guide to Old Time Catfish Techniques
Pocket Guide to Field Dressing, Butchering & Cooking Deer
Pocket Guide to Bowhunting Whitetail Deer
Pocket Guide to Spring & Fall Turkey Hunting
Guide to Fishing, Hunting & Camping Truman
The Pro's Guide to Fishing Missouri Lakes
Waterfowling, A Sportsman's Handbook
Modern Waterfowl Hunting
Shotgunner's Guide
Gun Care and Repair
Outdoorsman's Fix-It Book
Outdoorsman's Workshop
Building and Equipping the Garden and Small Farm Workshop
Basic House Wiring
Complete Guide to Building Log Homes
Children's Toys and Furniture
64 Yard and Garden Projects You Can Build
How to Build 50 Classic Furniture Reproductions
Tile Indoors and Out
The Home Cabinetmaker
How to Build Small Barns & Outbuildings
Masonry & Concrete
Pole Building Projects
Building Small Barns, Sheds & Shelters
Home Canning & Preserving (w/Joan Burch)
Building Mediterranean Furniture (w/Jay Hedden)
Fireplaces (w/Robert Jones)
The Homeowner's Complete Manual of Repair and Improvement (w/3 others)
The Good Earth Almanac Series
Survival Handbook
Old-Time Recipes
Natural Gardening Handbook

THE ULTIMATE GUIDE TO SKINNING AND TANNING

A Complete Guide to Working with Pelts, Fur, and Leather

Monte Burch

The Lyons Press

An imprint of the Globe Pequot Press

Guilford, Connecticut

The Lyons Press is an imprint of The Globe Pequot Press.

Printed in the United States of America

10 9 8 7 6 5 4 3 2 1

Library of Congress Cataloging-in-Publication Data is available on file.

ISBN 1-58574-670-3

Contents

Introduction   vii

Chapter 1—Understanding Tanning   1

Chapter 2—Tools and Workplace   17

Chapter 3—Tanning Formulas and Materials   41

Chapter 4—Skinning Small Game, Furbearers
and Predators   63

Chapter 5—Skinning Deer, Big Game and
Domestic Animals   83

Chapter 6—Preserving and Storing Hides and Pelts   103

Chapter 7—Tanning Small Game and Furbearers   125

Chapter 8—Modern Methods of Tanning Deer and
Big Game Hides   149

Chapter 9—Making Buckskin   175

Chapter 10—Tanning Domestic Hides and Skins and
Hair-On Robes   193

Chapter 11—Rawhide, Latigo and Sole Leather   207

Chapter 12—Birds   211

Chapter 13—Skinning and Preserving Reptiles   219

Source List   231

Index   233

Introduction

Home tanning of hides, furs and skins is very interesting and fun. Home tanning provides a way of utilizing hides and furs for any number of items, including clothing, accessories and decorator items. The tanning information in this book ranges from the most primitive to the latest in modern materials and methods. Buckskinners may wish to try their hand at creating traditional buckskin for clothing. Buckskin is one of the oldest forms of tanning and requires little in the way of materials or tools. The strength of your back is the major ingredient in tanning buckskin.

Modern tanning methods, even those used by commercial tanners, can also be done at home with a few tools, many of which you can make yourself. Utilizing modern materials can be quite scientific, while some of the older formulas and methods are more "art" than science. It is, however, fun to experiment with all the different methods.

Tanning is a learning process. You will probably make a few mistakes. The formulas and methods in this book are fairly standard. The results, however, can't be guaranteed due to the wide number of variables involved.

Some tanning methods involve caustic or poisonous materials. It's important to always handle, store, use and dispose of these materials in a safe manner.

Tanning is hard physical work, but it can be very relaxing work. Also, quite a bit of time is needed for many of the tanning methods. It can, however, be extremely satisfying to produce a beautiful and usable leather or fur pelt.

Understanding Tanning

Tanning is one of the oldest skills of mankind. Tanning, or the manufacture of leather, is also still one of the most important trades of the modern day. Tanning can be complicated, or it can be simple. The simplest primitive tanning methods used nothing more than animal fats and lots of hard work to preserve the hide, which was then stretched to soften it and smoked to further preserve it. Historically, vegetable and chemical tanning followed the primitive method. The Romans were very adept at tanning, and by the Middle Ages tanneries were quite common.

The first step in tanning is to acquire animal, bird or reptile hides or skins. Almost any critter can be used, but the skin must be fresh. As soon as the creature dies, putrefaction sets in. For this reason the carcass must be skinned immediately after killing. Do not use skins from animals that have died from natural causes and have been dead for some time.

Skins and hides are never perfect. Damage often occurs from animals fighting each other. Warble flies, which lay eggs just beneath the surface of the skin, can cause

1

Tanning is one of mankind's oldest skills, and a skill that is just as important today. Home tanning is not particularly complicated, but it does take work.

holes in the hide. Tick and other insect bites can cause skin imperfections. Bullet or arrow holes are found on animals that are hunted or trapped. Damage may also occur during the skinning process. It's very important to carefully skin the animals as soon as possible and take great care not to cut through the hide during the process. Some holes can be sewn, but the results are not the same as a good, solid skin. Other common imperfections include growth marks on large, mature animals, particularly on the upper portion of the neck. These "wrinkles" make tanning those hides harder.

HIDES OR SKINS

Hides are from older and/or larger animals, such as cows, bulls, elk, buffalo, hogs and horses. Skins are from younger and/or smaller animals, such as deer, sheep, goats and calves. Skins are from furbearing wild animals as well.

Hides and skins are graded according to weight:

Bulls	.60 lbs. and up
Mature Cows and Steers	.60 lbs. and up
Two-Year-Old Calves	.40 to 60 lbs.
Elk	.40 to 60 lbs.
Buffalo	.80 lbs. and up
Bear	.25 to 60 lbs.
Deer	.10 to 20 lbs.
Sheep and Goats	.10 to 15 lbs.

Skins for furs should be taken in the winter months when the fur is thickest and at its best. Hides and skins for leather should be taken in the summer months, or before the winter hair growth removes many of the nutrients from the skin. The lesser amount of hair also makes it easier to remove the hair for leather.

The different species produce different types of hides and skins. Cow and bull hides produce the most commonly available commercial leathers. These hides may be shaved or split into thinner hides for other uses as well. Horse and mule hides are somewhat coarser grained and are best used for harness leather, belting and heavy leathers, as well as for rawhide products. Moose and elk hides can be used for a wide variety of purposes. The lighter skins, including deer and goat, can be used for

Skins may be tanned into buckskin and leather using ancient methods.

shoes or moccasins, gloves, clothing and accessories. Both goat and deer skins are fine grained and fairly thin and are also fairly easy to tan.

Cow, bull and buffalo can also be tanned with the hair on for robes or rugs. Furbearer skins can be used for coats, caps, gloves and accessories. Sheepskin can be tanned with the wool on for unusual garments. Other exotic skins include reptile, shark and bird skins.

PRESERVING

Ideally, the tanning process should begin as soon as the hide or skin is removed from the animal. In many instances, however, the hide will be preserved and tanned at a later date. The hide must be preserved properly until the tanning process. The simplest and oldest method is to dry the hide. The dried hide must not be allowed to get wet. These naturally dried skins, however, do not make a good-quality leather, although the method is common for fur pelts.

Salting the skin is a traditional method of preserving. Skins to be shipped are often brined in a salt solution, keeping the skins constantly moving and continually adding salt to the solution. Once the brine penetrates the skins, they are removed and allowed to dry.

Dry salting is the most common preserving method for home tanners. Salt is sprinkled over the flesh side of the skin, then the skin is hung up to dry or laid out. Skins can be kept for several months with this method. If a number of skins are to be preserved, the salt is sprinkled on the flesh side of one skin, a second skin is placed on top of the first and salted, and the process repeated until all the hides are salted.

Sheep skins are often pickled in a salt and acid pickling solution.

Another preserving method is to simply freeze the skin or hide. This does require freezer space, and large skins can take up a lot of space, especially if left with the hair on. Skins can also become freezer burned if left too long. It's best to flesh the hide before freezing; although hides can be fleshed after freezing, it is more difficult. Simply roll the hide up in a ball, place in a plastic garbage bag and place in the freezer. Be sure to label the package.

HIDE STRUCTURE

In order to understand the process of tanning, you must first understand the structure of the hides. Skin is made up of several layers, with the epidermis the upper or outer surface layer. The epidermis consists mostly of dead cells that have hardened. The dermis layer lies next, and it consists of three separate layers: grain, junction and corium. Each of these layers contains densely interwoven fibers made up of a protein called collagen. These fiber bundles are what make leather so unique. The grain layer is the topmost of the derma layers and consists of extremely dense but fine bundles of fibers.

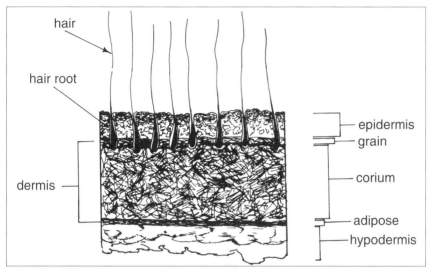

labels: hair, hair root, dermis, epidermis, grain, corium, adipose, hypodermis

The skin is made up of several layers; understanding the different layers is important to proper tanning.

The corium lies below with more pronounced and larger fiber bundles, positioned at different angles from the grain layer. Called the "angle of weave," these angles differ to some extent with the different species of animals, birds, or reptiles.

Between the grain and corium is the junction layer. The adipose membrane is next to the hypodermis, and the bottom or inside flesh layer is the hypodermis. This flesh layer contains meat and fat, which must be removed.

The skin also contains the sebaceous glands, which secrete oils to lubricate the hair and skin, and sudoriferous glands or sweat glands. The erector pili muscles in the skin raise the hair. The skin also contains either hair

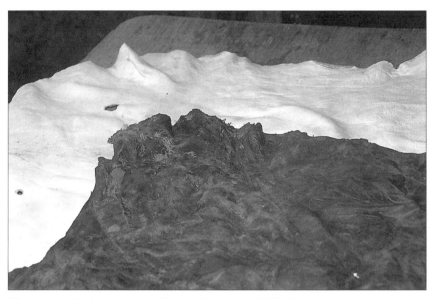

Modern methods and materials may also be used. The leather in the background was tanned with commercial acid tanning materials, the foreground with a chrome tanning technique.

or wool. The hair grows through the skin in the follicle with the hair root lying at the base of the follicle. The follicles are actually tiny holes in the skin, and on pigskin the follicles are quite pronounced. You can actually see the hair holes from the bottom of the skin on pigskin.

Understanding the structure of skin is important in order to understand the tanning process. The first step is to remove all the layers of skin that do not contain the fiber bundles—except for hair-on tanning, in which case the upper layers are not disturbed. This removal is done by scraping. The scraping procedure consists of three

Skins may also be tanned with the hair on for wall hangings, rugs and even hats and garments.

steps: fleshing, or removing all flesh, meat and fat from the underside of the skin; graining, or removing all hair, the epidermis and the upper grain from the top of the skin; and membraning, which removes the weaker membranes and further relaxes the fiber bundles.

Once the unwanted materials are removed, the next step is to preserve or stabilize the skin and prevent the proteins in the collagen from putrefying. Drying halts the putrefaction process somewhat but produces a hard, rigid skin, such as rawhide. If the skin is allowed to get wet again, the putrefaction process continues. The process of tanning turns the skin into a dry but flexible material that can undergo repeated wetting and drying without decay. This is done by modifying the chemical structure of the proteins to make them less soluble in water and inhibiting molecular cohesion to create a flexible material.

HIDE TERMINOLOGY

Because different parts of hides are used for different types of leather, these parts have specific names in commercial tanning.

Sides: Large hides are split down the middle to produce two sides.

Butt or Bend: Area of the best quality and most consistent leather.

Neck: Thickest portion of the leather, but often contains creases and growth marks.

Shoulder: Weaker than the neck or butt, but still quality leather.

Backbone: Thinner than the neck or butt.

Belly: The thinnest portion of the hide. It also has less dense fiber structure.

Flank: The thinnest and weakest portion of the hide.

Shanks: Skin from the legs, quite often removed before tanning, especially on smaller skins.

Tail: Also often removed unless the hide is to be for a robe or rug.

Crop: The head, shoulder and butt of a hide side.

Back: A butt or bend and shoulder.

Tanning Terminology

Tanning has its own terminology. Some terms are mostly related to commercial tanning, but others apply to home tanning. Knowing the terms makes it easier to understand the processes.

Bark Tannage: Leather tanned with the tannins contained in the bark of trees.

Chrome Tannage: Leather tanned with chromium salts.

Combination Tannage: Leather tanned with chrome and tree bark tannins.

Cowhide: Leather made from the hides of cows.

Full Grain: Leather with an unaltered grain or dermis layer.

Grain: The natural texture of leather.

Heavy Leather: Unsplit cattle hides used for soles, belts and straps.

Hide: The pelt of a large animal.

Kip: The hide of a grass-fed, young bovine.

Leather: A preserved and dressed animal hide.

Liming: Removal of the hair in preparing hides for tanning.

Oak Tannage: Originally almost all leather was tanned with oak bark tannin, but now means any bark tannin.

Papillary: Upper portion of hide, separated from reticular or split layer.

Rawhide: Untanned or partially tanned hides.

Side: One half of a hide split down the backbone.

Shave: After tanning, excess thickness is removed from the bottom side of the leather by a shaving machine.

Skive: Reduce leather to a specific thickness by shaving, slicing or peeling.

Split Leather: The bottom split or reticular layer of hide, which contains no natural grain.

Strap Leather: Heavyweight, industrial leather, tanned with tannin.

Suede: Fibrous leather made from the reticular.

Tannin: Astringent plant substances used in tanning leather.

Vegetable Tanning: Tanning leather with plant tannin.

TANNING STEPS

Regardless of commercial or home tanning, specific steps must be taken to ensure a properly tanned hide or pelt. The same basic steps are taken regardless of the type of skin, or end result. Naturally, hair-on pelts and rugs do not require some of the steps. Following are the basic tanning steps.

1. Skinning: The very first step is skinning the animal. Skinning of the different species is described in the following chapters.
2. Fleshing: This is one of the most important steps. All fat, meat and membranes must be removed from the flesh side of the skin.
3. Preserving: The hides are preserved by air drying, salting, freezing or a combination of the methods.
4. Soaking: Regardless of whether the skins have been air dried, salt dried, frozen or a combination, the

first step is to soak them in clean water. Detergent, salt and a biocide may also be added, depending on the type of skin. This is also called "relaxing" the skin.

5. Liming: Skins to be made into leather without the hair or fur are soaked in a lime solution. This causes the breakdown of keratin, the main protein of hair, as well as dissolves the hair root and epidermis. Liming does not damage the collagen or dermis portion of the skin, but it does remove the fibrillary proteins and causes osmotic and lyotropic swelling and plumping. In effect the dermis becomes swollen and engorged with water, opening the fiber bundles for a more thorough penetration of the tanning materials. Liming can take from just a day or two to a week or more depending on the weather and temperature.

6. Dehairing: Scrapers are used to scrape the hair and epidermis from the top surface of the skin.

7. Neutralizing: The liming step causes the skins to become alkaline. The skins are soaked in water to which lactic acid or vinegar is added to bring down the alkalinity and wash the lime materials away. This step may be only an hour or so for small skins to several hours for larger skins.

8. Pickling: Soaking the skin in a pickling solution also helps to neutralize the alkaline, kills bacterial growth and is used to hold the skin until it can be tanned. Hides without hair are normally held two to three days.

9. Shaving and Scudding: Thick skins, or the thick areas of some skins, are commonly shaved on the back side to create more uniformity and make it easier for the chemicals to penetrate. Scudding is running a blunt scraper over the grain side to remove any remaining hair root, skin pigmentation and surface fat.

10. Second Pickling: The skins are then returned to the pickle bath so the exposed areas can be pickled, and held in the pickle until tanned. Keep in the pickle bath at least 24 hours.

11. Degreasing: Some skins, such as raccoon and bear, must be degreased.

12. Second Neutralizing: The skins are again soaked in a neutralizing bath.

13. Tanning: The skins are tanned using one of the tanning formulas. This can take a few hours to several days or months depending on the materials used.

14. Rinse: Rinse the tanning materials from the skin.

15. Oiling: While the skin is still fairly wet, rub oil into the back side of the skin.

16. Drying and Softening: Allow the skin to dry, which may take a few hours for small skins to several days for larger skins. As the skin begins to dry, soften it by rubbing over a stake, by attaching it to a stake frame and using a shoulder stake, or by pulling around a rope or cable.

17. Finishing: After the skin dries it can also be thinned and made more supple by sanding, rasping or wire wheeling the back side. Furs should be dried, fluffed and combed using cornmeal or sawdust.

Tools and Workplace

A t best, tanning hides and furs is messy, and it's often smelly as well. Most of the work is best done outside; however, direct sunlight and high heat can create tanning problems with some skins. If working outside, shade should be provided. A handy shade tree works quite well, and can be rigged with a gambrel for skinning. Saplings, ropes and cables as well as other ways can also be rigged to help in the stretching and drying processes. Most tanning tools can be purchased, but you can also make many of the tools quite easily.

More important is a safe place for storage of the tubs of chemicals. Many of these chemicals are poisonous or dangerous to children, pets and wild animals. Make sure these operations are done in a safe place. You should also have a dry, lockable area for storing the different chemicals and such things as lime, salt and so forth.

An inside working area is important for cold weather. This inside area can also be used for some of the final steps in tanning, as well as for storing stretched hides to be tanned. The area should have good ventilation and be well lighted but provide storage safe from pets and varmints that may chew or ruin pelts. Regardless of the location, water should be available.

Outside Tools

A skinning pole is handy for hanging game and critters to skin. This can be as simple as a tree limb, or an elaborate pole. I have a butchering and skinning area out behind my barn. The area started with a discarded refrigerator truck body that I use for cooling game in hot weather. A skinning pole is lashed from the top of the cooler to a pair of cross support poles.

For big game you'll also need a hoist. Gambrels to match the size of the game from big game to small game are necessary. An outside skinning table can also be a great help for skinning small game and birds. Just about any solid table will work. It should, however, be fairly high so you don't have to stoop over to work. The surface should also be easily cleaned.

A fleshing beam is necessary for scraping flesh and hair from hides. This can be constructed for inside use,;however, because of the mess, I prefer an outside beam for the larger hides such as deer or cow. The beam should be sized to the most common usage. A large beam, approximately 2 feet in diameter and about 8 feet long, would be best for a cow, moose or elk hide. However, a beam 10 to 12 inches in diameter would suffice. A deer skin fleshing beam can be 8 to 10 inches in diameter by 6 feet long. A deer skin, however, can be worked on the larger beam used for cow hides.

I made my outside beam quite simply from a section of sycamore tree. The wood choice is because sycamore doesn't have thick bark, and it can easily be smoothed up with just a bit of work with a draw knife. The high end of

A good workplace is extremely important. For skinning game you'll need a game pole, hoists and gambrels.

A lot of tanning is messy, especially dehairing. An outside workplace is helpful.

the beam should be at a comfortable working height for you. I like mine just under my chest. Smaller-sized skins are more easily fleshed on smaller-sized fleshing beams, so you may need more than one beam, including an outside and inside beam.

A stretching frame is needed for stretching hides in brain tanning buckskin and other leathers, as well as for stretching hides to dry into rawhide. This frame can be assembled of 2 x 4s, but I made mine of 2-inch saplings lashed together. Sturdy ⅛-inch nylon cord is used to stretch the skins on the frame. The frame can be stood up inside a garage or shed or under a shade tree for use. The stretching process for brain tanning hides can also be done with a piece of cable or heavy rope anchored to two

A fleshing beam is necessary for dehairing and fleshing hides. An outside beam is best for dehairing. Note that the beam shown also has a staking tool attached for outside leather softening.

Author's fleshing beam is made of a sycamore log. Bark is removed and the beam smoothed with a draw knife.

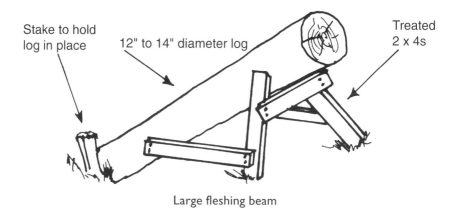

Stake to hold log in place

12" to 14" diameter log

Treated 2 x 4s

Large fleshing beam

A stretching frame is used for stretching hides for buckskin tanning.

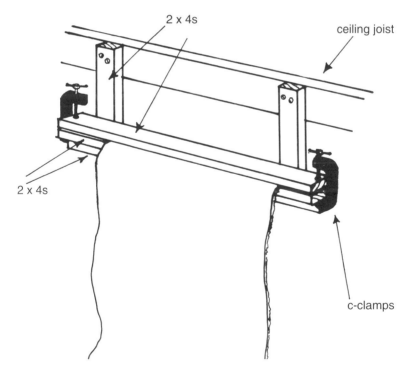

2 x 4s

ceiling joist

2 x 4s

c-clamps

A tanner's frame can be used to stretch and soften hides.

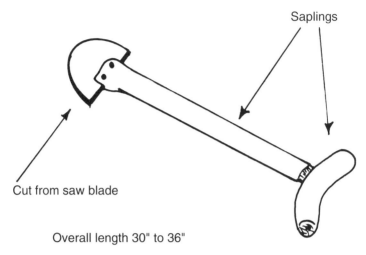

Saplings

Cut from saw blade

Overall length 30" to 36"

A shoulder stake is used with the frame.

solid locations. A tanner's frame can also be made for either inside or outside use. It consists of two upright 2 x 4s with two boards fashioned between that can be used to clamp one end of the hide in place. A shoulder knife or "stake" is then used to break the hide. A simple tanner's frame for outside can consist of posts set in the ground, or you can make an assembled frame for inside use.

If drying rawhide or beaver skins in the round, a board, such as a piece of plywood and roofing nails, can be used to hold the hides until they dry.

Fur stretchers are needed for small game pelts. These can be purchased wire stretchers, or you can make your own from solid wood. If you're doing a fairly large number of animals, you'll probably prefer the metal stretchers as they don't take up as much storage room. Different-sized

Fur stretchers are needed for drying and preserving pelts. Metal frames are common. They're economical and take up little room.

animals require different-sized stretchers. Shown are the most common sizes. Cut these to shape from a solid piece of wood. White pine shelving lumber is fairly economical and easy to work with. Cut with a saber or bandsaw then round all edges and smooth with sandpaper so the frames won't catch on or cut the skins. With the wooden stretchers you'll need a method of slightly stretching the hide so it can be removed once it has cured on the stretching board. A tapered wooden wedge is usually placed against one side of the board. Once the pelt has dried, the wedge can then be removed and the hide more easily slipped off. Stickpins are also needed to pin the hide to the board. The stretched furs should be hung from a ceiling with fur hangers to hold the stretchers—or nails in the ceiling will suffice. Tail strippers can make the chore of stripping the hide from the tailbone much easier.

You'll need lots of tubs and tanks for soaking hides in the various solutions. Large plastic tubs are the best choice. For really large hides such as elk, moose or cow, plastic stock watering tanks, such as those from Rubbermaid, are excellent. They're sturdy, easy to clean and lightweight. Plastic barrels are also great for this chore. Hangers should be made for the larger tanks and barrels to suspend the hides and keep them from folding over and creating untanned areas in the folds. Hangers can be made of broomstick material, or saplings, suspended from the top of the tank or barrel with ropes. Do not use metal buckets or tubs, as most of the chemicals used are highly corrosive to metal.

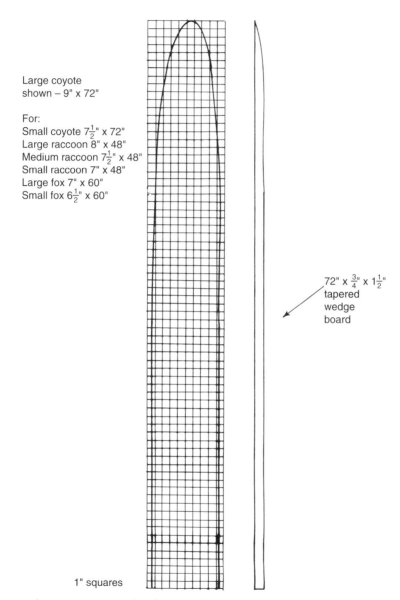

Large coyote
shown – 9" x 72"

For:
Small coyote $7\frac{1}{2}$" x 72"
Large raccoon 8" x 48"
Medium raccoon $7\frac{1}{2}$" x 48"
Small raccoon 7" x 48"
Large fox 7" x 60"
Small fox $6\frac{1}{2}$" x 60"

72" x $\frac{3}{4}$" x $1\frac{1}{2}$"
tapered
wedge
board

1" squares

You can make your own wooden fur stretchers.

You will need lots of tubs and tanks for soaking hides.

INSIDE AND OTHER TOOLS

Several of the tanning steps can also be done inside. Actually all of the steps can be done inside. When fleshing small animals, an inside fleshing beam may be preferred. The inside beam can be the same design as the beam shown for outside, except smaller. Shown opposite is a beam constructed of pressure-treated lumber for inside or outside use. A small fleshing beam can also be fastened vertically or horizontally to the tanning workbench. A small fleshing beam can even be fastened to a wall and hinged to swing up out of the way when not in use. For inside fleshing, or dehairing, a tub or bucket should be

An inside and smaller fleshing beam can be used in inclement weather and is important for small game. The beam shown is made from a pressure-treated 2 x 6 and anchored to a workbench with screws.

kept under the beam to catch the scrapings. Cardboard can also be put down on the floor and then discarded when it becomes too "messy."

A sturdy workbench is extremely important. The workbench will be used for many tanning steps including holding breaking or stretching stakes for drawing or pulling hides. A carpenter's vise can be used to hold the stakes. Drawers and shelves under the bench, or a cabinet is needed for holding smaller items such as knives and scrapers. A pair of sawhorses and a piece of ⅜-inch plywood sheathing is handy for laying out hides to salt or for dry tan.

First step is to round the end with a saber or bandsaw. Then use a draw knife to round the top.

Several different sizes of breaking stakes are needed for the different-sized skins. These stakes are cut from 1X and 2X materials. As described, these can be held in a carpenter's vise, or fastened permanently to the tanning bench. I fastened one to my outside fleshing beam for outside work. You can also set a wooden post outside in the ground and shape the top end into a breaking stake. In all instances the stakes should have rounded corners and the top edge should be tapered. A piece of ⅛-inch-thick metal, with the corners rounded and the edge smooth, can be inset in the top of the breaking stake and provides more of an edge for working larger hides such as deer skins.

Finally, smooth up the top and edge surfaces with a belt sander.

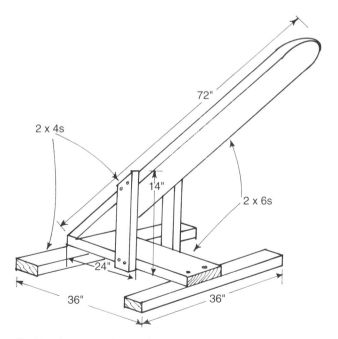

A stand-up fleshing beam can be made.

If you intend to do quite a bit of tanning, a breaking bench can make the chore a little easier. A breaking bench consists of a bench on which you sit, with a stake fastened in one end. The breaking end of the stake can be tapered wood, or a piece of heavy crosscut saw blade material cut, rounded and inserted into the top edge. The latter is better for the heavier skins, the former for thinner, more easily torn skins such as small game and predators.

You'll also need small tubs, buckets, and measuring cups for holding and measuring chemicals. Again, these should all be nonmetallic. A scale is necessary for weighing hides, as well as for weighing some chemicals or materials used in the tanning process. It's important to maintain the proper pH with some solutions. Paper strips for testing pH are necessary, along with salinometer for

A breaking stake can also be used for stretching and softening hides.

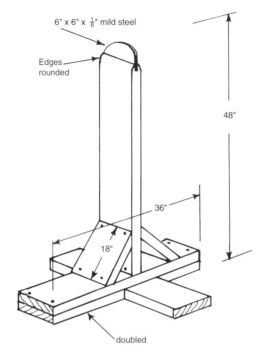

Breaking stake assembled from 2 x 6 treated lumber.

testing salt content. Long wooden stirring sticks or paddles are necessary for stirring the hides around in the solutions as well as for lifting the hides back out.

Slickers are used to push and stretch hides for breaking, and they can be made of wood or wood with a metal edge. Indian slickers were actually made of flint. Wooden slickers can be made, or you can inset a metal blade for better performance. Scudding knives are slickers with a concave blade so they can be used on the fleshing beam.

A wide assortment of knives is extremely important. Skinning knives, both large and small, with their rounded

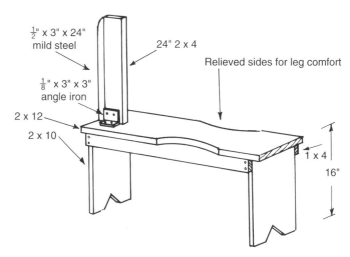

Breaking stakes can be tiring on the shoulders. A breaking bench offers the chance to sit down and do the same job.

Measuring devices and scales are also necessary.

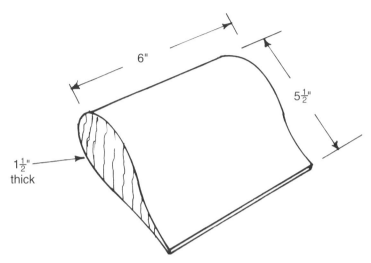

6"

5½"

1½"
thick

Slickers are used to soften heavy leathers.

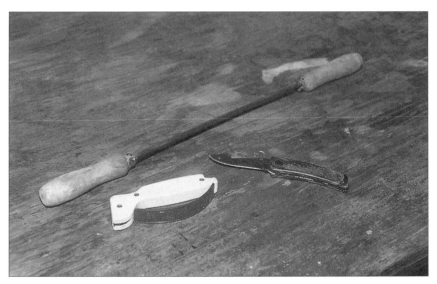

A skinning knife, fleshing knife and sharpener are the basic tools for tanning hides.

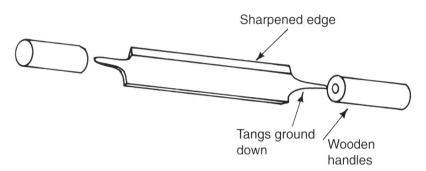

You can make your own fleshing knife from an old file.

points, are needed for skinning the different types of game or domestic animals. Sharper-pointed knives are also important for cutting hides, trimming and other chores. A pelting knife, which has a short, sharp blade, is handy for skinning small furred game.

Scrapers, or fleshing knives, are necessary for removing the flesh and dehairing the hide. Native Americans

If you want to be authentic, Native American artifacts can be used. Shown are two hide scrapers.

used flint or bone scrapers. I've found several of these ancient scrapers roaming the Ozark hills near my home. Deer, elk or buffalo femur or rib bones were also used for fleshing or dehairing. Notches were cut in the end of the femur bone, while the rib bone has the concave surface sharpened so it can be used over a log or fleshing beam. These are still a good choice for fleshing thin hides such as small game. A wooden, L-shaped scraper can also be used for this chore. The Native Americans also inset flint or metal scrapers into elk antlers. Carpenter's draw knives can be used for fleshing knives if you blunt the edge so it's flat, like a skate blade. Or you can purchase manufactured fleshing knives. Purchased fleshing knives are the easiest to use, as they don't cut the

Or you can make more modern tools. Shown are a stretcher and scraper.

smaller hides, yet have enough "bite" to work the larger hides. They are available with a concave surface to fit the convex surface of fleshing beams. You can also make your own fleshing knife from an old rasp or file. One side can be ground to an edge for fleshing, and the opposite left flat for dehairing. A scraper can also be made from a piece of bent sapling and a rounded metal blade. A purchased skiving knife can be used to thin down thick portions of hides. The best tactic for this, however, is a wooden block and sandpaper or a wood-working rasp. A shoulder stake, using a piece of ⅛-inch-thick metal inset in a handle, offers another method of breaking or staking hides.

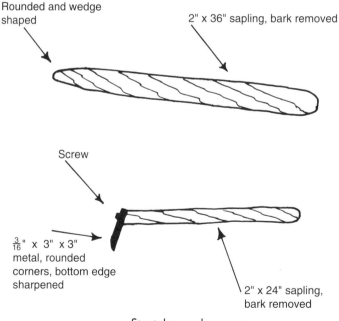

Stretcher and scraper.

Sharpening tools are needed for sharpening skinning and other knives. A power hone such as one from Chef's Choice makes the chore quick and easy. One of the handiest sharpeners I've seen is the Intruder. It's great for the quick touch-up of blades. I keep one by my hand while skinning, fleshing or other tanning chores.

Scrub brushes and towels are important necessities. A waterproof apron is needed to protect your clothing and your body from chemicals. Furrier's combs and curry combs are needed for cleaning and brushing out furs. A needle and heavy-duty waxed thread can be used to sew up holes in hides.

If you intend to try a vegetable tan with bark or other natural ingredients, you'll need a grinder to grind the materials. A chipper shredder can be used for the initial

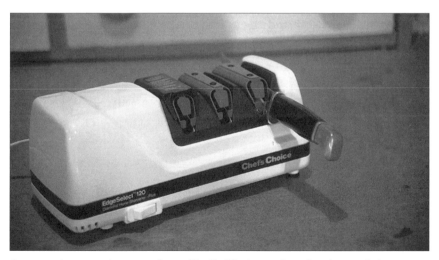

A power hone such as one from Chef's Choice makes the chore of sharpening knives quick and easy.

grinding. Or you can chop the bark into small pieces with a hatchet, then run it through a feed mill, or hand-cranked grain mill.

Two other items are not absolutely necessary, but will make some of the tanning chores easier. An old wringer washing machine is great for squeezing the water and tanning solutions out of the hides. An old electric clothes dryer, without the heating element, can be used to tumble and clean hair-on hides. Or you can make a wooden tumbler and power it with an electric motor.

SAFETY

It's extremely important to wear protective latex gloves when skinning and handling untanned animal skins, or especially when brain tanning deer skins. Diseases from animals can be transmitted through a cut on your hands or even chapped hands. Either disposable vinyl or latex gloves may be used. The gloves don't have to be discarded after one use if they're sound and not nicked or cut. Sprinkle a bit of baby powder inside and you can slip them off and on fairly easy, even used gloves. When you're through skinning, or handling the raw hides or furs, wash your hands in warm, soapy water using an antibacterial soap with just a small amount of hydrogen peroxide added to the water to disinfect your hands. Eye protection, waterproof apron, long-sleeved shirts, long pants and sturdy shoes are all needed when handling some caustic materials.

CHAPTER

3

Tanning Formulas and Materials

Any number of formulas and materials have been and can be used for tanning. Hides and skins can be tanned with nothing more than animal brains, fats, or oils, along with lots of hard work. A variety of materials, however, can be used for tanning different types of furs or hides. Many of these are ordinary household chemicals, or natural materials. Some old-time materials, though effective, are dangerous and environmental hazards. These days many manufactured tanning formulas are also available, even to home tanners, and they do a better job in most instances.

WATER

Water is used in many of the tanning steps. Although just about any kind of water can be used, the best choice is rainwater or water that doesn't contain high amounts of materials such as lime, which can create tanning problems.

SALT

Regardless of the tanning process, salt is one of the most commonly used materials. Salt is used to preserve the skin and prepare it for tanning, as well as used in conjunction with other materials for the tanning process. Noniodized sodium chloride or salt is available at local grocery stores, but you can purchase larger bags at a more economical price at the local feed stores. Ordinary stock salt is coarser than table salt, but the coarseness isn't a problem with most tanning. In most tanning methods, about 1 pound of salt is required for each pound of skin, regardless of the processing step.

RELAXING BATH SOLUTION

Hides that have been frozen, dried or salted to preserve them should first be soaked in a relaxing solution made by dissolving 1 ounce of borax to each gallon of warm water needed to cover the hide.

DEHAIRING SOLUTIONS

The hair or fur can be removed from hides with several formulas. Wood ashes are a very common material used for the purpose. Wood ashes mixed with water produce a lye that loosens the hair. The ashes should be white, and not contain the black chunks of charcoal left from cleaning out the fireplace. It's best to sieve out the black charcoal pieces because they can stain the hide. Either soft-wood or hardwood ashes may be used, although softwood ashes tend to be somewhat weaker and the dehairing process takes longer. You'll need about 3 gallons of ashes to do a hide. Keep the ashes stored in a dry place until you're ready to use them, as water will leach out the lye. Add approximately 1½ gallons of ashes to each 5 gallons of water, creating enough of the mixture to cover the hide. Stir the ashes thoroughly, then place an egg in the solution. The egg should float. If not, add more ashes.

The old-timers created lye for use in tanning and also for making soap for tanning by leaching out the wood ashes. The ashes were placed in a wooden barrel with

A number of chemicals are required for tanning. Salt and lime are needed in large quantities.

holes drilled around the sides, and water was poured in the barrel. Two 5-gallon plastic tubs can be substituted for the barrel. Drill drain holes in one and place it over the second with wood strips to support it. Place a 5-inch layer of straw in the top tub, then fill the tub with ashes. Pour water on the ashes. Each day pour on more water as the water is absorbed. When the bottom tub is full of lye water, remove the solution and boil it until a piece of raw potato will float in it. Purchased lye can also be used, with ¼ cup lye added to 10 gallons of water.

Hydrated builder's or caustic lime can also be used, and usually produces a faster, easier and more consistent process. Mix 1 pint of lime to each gallon of water. Lime is also available at farm stores.

Neutralizing Formulas

Once the hair has been removed, the hide should be placed in a neutralizing solution. One neutralizing solution consists of 1 gallon of vinegar to 3 gallons of water. Or 6 ounces of lactic acid powder to 3 gallons of water can be used.

Pickling Formulas

Pickling acidifies the skin and kills bacterial growth. Pickling can also be used to hold the skin safely until it can be conveniently shaved, degreased, washed and rinsed or tanned. Return the skin to the pickle between steps and prior to placing in the tanning solution. Pickling is a temporary preservative, but it is not tanning. After shaving, always return the skin to the pickle for two days because shaving exposes and opens areas of the skin not previously pickled.

The following formulas are the basic standard formulas most commonly used throughout the tanning industry. The amounts given are for each gallon of water required to cover the skin or skins totally immersed. In addition to the specific acid, 1 pound of salt is required for each gallon of water. All pickles should be stirred at least once or twice daily and should be kept at a temperature of 65 to 80 degrees F. The pH should also be checked frequently.

½ fl. oz. (4½ level teaspoons) Saftee-Acid
1 oz. concentrated sulphuric acid
1 oz. oxalic acid crystals
1.1 oz. (by weight) 85% formic acid
2 oz. acetic acid 56%
3 oz. citric acid
4 oz. sodium bisulphate
12.8 oz. aluminum sulphate *or* 12.8 oz. ammonium aluminum sulphate *or* 12.8 oz. potassium aluminum sulphate
1 oz. muriatic acid (HCL)
4 oz. new, unused battery acid

In addition to the above pickles, a white vinegar pickle can also be made with 2 quarts white vinegar,

2 quarts water and 1 pound salt in an amount needed to cover the immersed skin or skins.

Rittel's Saftee-Acid

Rittel's Saftee-Acid is one of the safest acids available. It provides a wide range of acidity with none of the disadvantages of other acids. Saftee-Acid is practically odorless, with no caustic fumes. It is nonpoisonous, has no dilution heat, is nonevaporative and is an excellent choice for pickling solutions as well as for adjusting pH levels.

A variety of tanning solutions may be made up of various chemicals—or some can be purchased ready to use.

Ordinary household chemicals can be used for some formulas and tanning steps.

PICKLING NEUTRALIZING SOLUTION

After the pickling process, the skins are neutralized again with a solution of 1 ounce sodium bicarbonate (baking soda) to every gallon of water needed to cover. Soak one hour.

Tanning Formulas

Tanning is done using six basic materials: brain or oil; soap or animal fat; chrome; acid; alum; and vegetable. Vegetable, brain or oil, and soap or animal fat tanning are ancient methods that still can be used with readily available natural materials. Chrome, acid and alum tanning are more modern methods, but require purchased materials. The method chosen also depends on the type of hide and the end results desired. The different types of tanning methods produce different results. The old methods also, for the most part, require more effort and time in the processes.

Brain Tanning

Brain tanning is a traditional method for creating buckskin, and requires only the brains from the animal killed. Or you can purchase brains from a slaughterhouse, or even order them through a local grocery store or butcher shop. Note: With the rise in chronic wasting disease (CWD) in many deer and elk herds, it is unwise to handle animal brains without wearing protective gloves. You might be better off purchasing domestic livestock brains. The fresh brains can be boiled and mixed into a slurry, then used, or simply frozen, for future use.

Oil Tanning

Animal fats or oils have also been a traditional tanning material. Pure neat's-foot oil is a very common tanning material. Egg yolks have also been used for tanning hair-on hides. Natural soap, made from animal tallow, has also been a traditional tanning material. Ivory Soap is a good substitute for natural soap. You'll need about two bars of soap per deer hide. Soap combined with lard can also be used. You can also make up your own soft soap with lye water and animal fats. You'll need one 13-ounce can of lye in flake form and 2½ pints of cold water, plus 6 pounds of rendered animal fat such as tallow or lard. Dissolve the lye in the water in a glass or plastic bowl. Stir slowly and be very careful: The lye is caustic and can cause severe burns. Wear protective eyewear any time you handle lye. If you should splash lye water on yourself, wash the area with plenty of cold water

Set the lye-water aside and melt the grease or fats to a clear liquid. Be careful not to allow the grease to catch afire. Pour the clear liquid through a kitchen strainer, then allow to cool until the liquid offers some resistance to stirring.

Bring both lye and grease to the temperatures shown on the chart, then very carefully pour the lye mixture into the melted grease in a steady thin stream. Stir constantly until the mixture reaches the consistency of thick honey. This should take about 10 to 15 minutes. Then pour the thickened soap into a wooden frame lined with a wet cotton sheet.

Cover the frame and soap with a clean board, then with newspapers, and an old blanket and allow to cool slowly. In about two weeks, remove the soap from the mold and cut into cakes.

Temperature Chart

Fat	Fat Temperature	Lye Temperature
Lard or soft fat	98–100 degrees F.	77–80 degrees F.
Half lard, half tallow	105–110 degrees F.	83–86 degrees F.
Tallow	125–130 degrees F.	93–96 degrees F.

Vegetable Bark Tanning

Barks and leaves containing tannin offer some of the most primitive but effective tanning materials. The oaks all offer good tanning materials, as do the sumacs, hemlock and chestnut. Tanning with these materials is an extremely slow process, sometimes requiring months. For this reason vegetable tanning is not normally used on furs, but is considered excellent for the heavy leathers such as harness leather.

The vegetable materials are best collected while the sap is rising, as the bark peels more readily from the trees at that time. The bark or materials should be stored in a dry place and allowed to dry thoroughly. They must then be shredded or ground into a fine dust. Initial shredding can be done with a chipper shredder. A feed grinder or stone meal grinder should be used for the final grinding. The materials are then steeped in hot water to create the tanning liquor.

Vegetable Extract Tanning

Modern vegetable tanning extracts are much quicker and easier than the old-time bark tanning method. These extracts tan in a week or so and include sumac and quebracho. Quebracho is one of the "catechols" or condensed tans. This is a very popular extract because it binds very quickly and strongly to a pelt. The resulting leather has a distinctively reddish brown color. Sumac, a pyrogallol, produces a leather with more of a yellow or greenish brown cast. It has a very deep tanning action and produces a mellow leather. Gambier is another popular vegetable extract. These are available in powder form to be mixed with water and are all available from Rittel's Tanning Supply.

Chemical Tanning

A wide variety of chemicals can be used alone, or mixed together to tan leather. Some chemicals are readily available around the home, or can be purchased fairly easily. Other chemicals are specialized.

Alum, in one form or another, is one of the most common chemicals. Combined with salt, alum is one of the most economical materials as well as one of the easiest for the beginner to use. Alum makes the tanned skin impervious to water and sets the epidermis and hair. Alum tanning produces a light-colored skin, but does not take repeated exposure to moisture very well. This type of tanning creates a fairly stiff hide that requires a great deal more staking than some other methods. Alum is available in several forms, including pure alum, which is available from drugstores. Industrial- or commercial-grade alum is less expensive. Potassium aluminum sulphate and ammonium aluminum sulphate are available from farm supply stores. One of the most effective is aluminum sulphate, a common garden chemical used for acid-loving plants and available at farm and garden supply stores. Following are some common alum formulas. Note: Alum is also caustic.

Salt-Alum Formula

2 gal. water
l lb. alum
2 lbs. salt

Slowly stir the alum, then the salt into warm water to dissolve. Bring to a boil to dissolve the materials, then allow to cool before using. Small, thin hides will usually tan in a couple of days; allow a week for larger hides.

Alum–Carbolic Acid

¼ lb. alum
½ oz. carbolic acid crystals
½ lb. salt
1 gallon water

Dissolve in warm water. Be cautious of carbolic acid crystals.

Salt-Alum Formula, Paste Tan

l lb. alum
1 qt. salt
¼ lb. saltpeter

Mix the ingredients together in a plastic bowl. Rub into a fleshed skin.

Alum-Vegetable

A combination alum-vegetable tan provides a tan with more of a traditional reddish or yellow pelt.

½ lb. salt
½ lb. aluminum sulphate

½ oz. gambier, sumac or quebracho extract
1 gallon water

Dissolve the extract in a quart of hot water. Dissolve the salt and aluminum sulphate in 3 quarts of water. Allow the extract water to cool and mix the two solutions together.

Acid tanning solutions are also quite common. Many of the recipes are old and have been replaced by more modern, safer and easier-to-use solutions.

Note: Most acids are poisonous and caustic. They can cause severe burns. The vapors should not be breathed, and plastic, non metal containers must be used. Wear rubber gloves, eye protection, a rubber apron, a long-sleeved shirt and long pants when working with any acids.

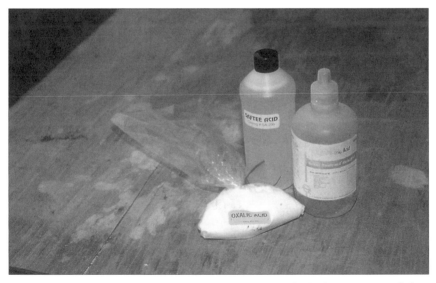

Other formulas call for specialized materials, some of which are caustic. Saftee Acid is a noncaustic substitute.

Sulphuric Acid

1 fluid oz. sulphuric acid (or 3 oz. sulphuric battery acid)
1 lb. salt
1 gal. water

Dissolve the salt in the water, then slowly pour the acid into the water, stirring the mixture as the acid is poured in. Thin- to medium-sized skins will take about three to four days.

Oxalic Acid

2 oz. oxalic acid crystals
¼ lb. salt
1 gal. water

Heat a quart of water and dissolve the acid crystals and salt in the warm water. Then pour in 3 quarts of water. Allow to cool before using. This a good formula for light to medium skins, and will tan in one to three days.

Sulphuric Acid Paste Formulas

1 oz. pure sulphuric acid (or 3 oz. sulphuric battery acid)
1 lb. salt

Mix the salt and acid together, then add just enough water to make a thin paste. Wearing rubber gloves, spread this over the flesh side of the skin, then cover the paste and skin with plastic garbage bags. Allow this to sit for six to eight hours, then remove the paste and apply a new layer. Allow this to dry without the plastic covering.

Alcohol-Turpentine Formula

This is a good choice for beginners and works well on small skins such as squirrel or rabbit.

½ pint wood alcohol
½ pint turpentine

Chrome Tanning

The most consistent tanning, especially for larger hides (30 pounds and heavier), is chrome tanning. Chrome

TANNIT from the Tandy Leather Company is ready to use and very easy.

tanning, however, is a bit more difficult, and the materials are harder to come by and dispose of properly. Chrome tanning tends to produce a leather with a bluish color. These hides are often dyed. Chrome tanning utilizes chromium potassium sulphate crystals.

Note: These crystals are poisonous and caustic. Wear protective clothing, eye protection, rubber gloves and apron.

Two separate mixtures are required for chrome tanning:

Mixture No. 1

1¾ lbs. sodium carbonate crystals
3 lbs. salt
1½ gals. water

Warm the water and mix in the salt and sodium carbonate, using a plastic container. Stir slowly to make sure all materials are dissolved.

Mixture No. 2

6 lbs. chromium potassium sulphate crystals
4½ gals. cold, soft water

These crystals are hard to dissolve. Stir until no crystals remain.

Once the ingredients have dissolved in both mixtures, slowly pour Mixture No. 1 into Mixture No. 2, stirring constantly to combine them. It should take 10 to 15 minutes of stirring to combine these mixtures properly.

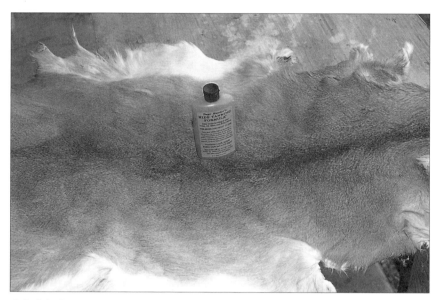

Cabela's Deer Hunter's Hide Tanning Formula is a pre-mixed product that is rubbed into the back of the skin for tanning.

This product is the basic chrome tanning liquor that is mixed with water to tan. The mixture is used in three separate batches, mixing a third of the mixture with 15 gallons of cold water.

Glutaraldehyde Tanning

The best-quality chemical tanned skin is with glutaraldehyde. The material, however, is somewhat harder to use, is more costly, and must be disposed of properly. Glutaraldehyde is an irritant. Avoid inhaling vapors as well as any contact with the skin. Wear rubber gloves, a rubber apron, and safety eye protection, and provide adequate ventilation.

For each pound of hide, prepare the following:
5 quarts water (approximately 85 degrees F.)
½ lb. technical-grade salt
2¼ fluid oz. glutaraldehyde (25% commercial solution)

Bring the water to approximately 85 degrees F. and pour into a wooden barrel or plastic garbage can. Add the salt and stir until dissolved. Pour the glutaraldehyde carefully into the salt solution and stir well.

COMMERCIAL TANNING FORMULAS

In addition to the "home brews," several "manufactured" tanning formulas and kits are available. Some are based on an oil-type tanning recipe, and some commercial tanning solutions are a "paste" or rub-on mixture rather than an immersion process. TANNIT, from Tandy Leather, is suitable for everything from deer hides to raccoon, coyote, bear, cowhides and even reptile, including alligator. One 16-ounce jar will process two deer hides. TANNIT is safe to use and has been fully approved by the Environmental Protection Agency. Independent laboratory reports confirm 99 percent penetration of TANNIT, even on thick unshaved cowhides. It is easy to use and doesn't require the space needed for the immersion methods.

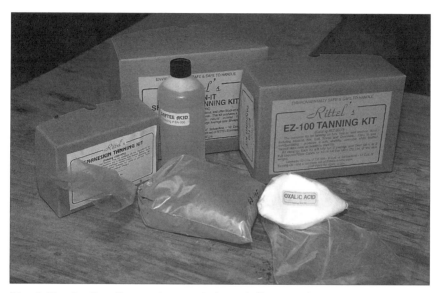

Rittel's Tanning Supplies carries a wide line of all types of tanning chemicals, materials and tools.

Cabela's Deer Hunter's Hide Tanning Formula is available in an 8-ounce bottle that will tan one deer hide or two fur skins. It is premixed and very easy to use.

Rittel's Tanning Supplies has a full line of all types of tanning materials, including their EZ-100 tanning material, a powdered Syntan tanning agent that eliminates environmental and personal handling problems. It costs less—and you use less—to tan more than many other products. It is a sulphonic acid agent synthetically manufactured and contains no metallic components. It is the easiest immersion tan product on the market and an excellent choice for garments, footwear and rugs.

Rittel's also carries a wide variety of oil as well as Chrome-Tan, Kwik-Tan, Kwik-N-Eze, a paint-on tan, Bird-Tan, Fish-Tan and Buckskin-Tan. A number of kits are available that include more of the materials needed for tanning.

OILING AND FINISHING

In many instances, the tanned hides are oiled and finished, a process that is normally done with animal oils. A sulphated neat's-foot oil solution is the most common.

For a single deer hide:
3½ oz. sulphated neat's-foot oil
3½ oz. warm water
1 oz. household ammonia

Oils are used to soften hides and make them more pliable.

Rittel's ProPlus Oil mixed 1 part oil with 2 parts hot tap water and applied to the skin while the oil is still hot is another oil alternative. The hot oil-water mixture is applied to the hide, the hide folded flesh-to-flesh and allowed to "sweat" in a warm area for four to six hours.

Disposal of Chemicals and Materials

Proper disposal of pickling and tanning solutions is extremely important. Some solutions are caustic and poisonous to humans, pets, livestock, and wildlife, as well as harmful to the soil. Check with local authorities on proper disposal.

CHAPTER 4

Skinning Small Game, Furbearers and Predators

Small game, furbearers and predators includes any number of critters that can provide either leather or furs. These animals are skinned in either of two ways—cased or open. Cased skinning is used if the skins are to be stretched on stretchers and dried for storage. In this method the skin is peeled off, like pulling a sock off wrong-side out. Open skinning is used if the skins are to be tanned immediately without stretching and drying, or are to be frozen for storage. An open skin actually has the skin opened up and stretched out to dry. Open-skin dressed furs can be used as wall hangings or rugs. Dried cased skins are opened up for use by draping over a fleshing beam and cutting the belly.

Small game can usually easily be skinned by laying the carcass belly-up on a table. A gambrel, suitable for skinning small game, makes the chore much easier. In a pinch, simply hang the animal up by tying a rope or string to a hind leg, and to a tree limb or other overhead object.

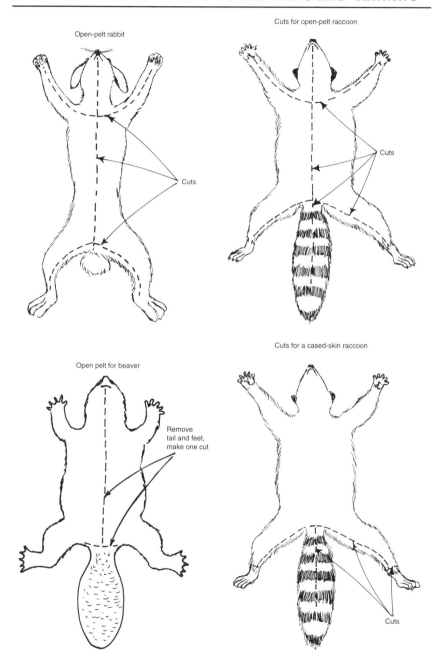

Open-pelt rabbit

Cuts for open-pelt raccoon

Cuts

Cuts

Open pelt for beaver

Remove
tail and feet,
make one cut

Cuts for a cased-skin raccoon

Cuts

Small game is skinned in one of two methods: open pelt or cased.

SMALL GAME

Small game includes rabbits, squirrels and groundhogs. Most are chosen and tanned for their pelts or fur. Some, such as rabbit, have extremely thin skin and can tear easily during the tanning process. Rabbit skin can be used as fur or for very fine leather. Groundhog, on the other hand, provides a very durable tanned leather. Groundhog was a common choice for rawhide with the Native Americans and settlers. Groundhogs are almost always open-hide skinned.

Rabbits

Rabbit skin, with the hair on, produces a great lining for gloves and mittens. Rabbits are commonly open skinned.

Small game can be skinned lying on a table.

The skin is very fragile and tears easily. To skin, make a cut from the anus to just under the chin. Be careful in making the cut along the belly, as the belly muscle is also very thin and you don't want to cut into the intestines and spill matter over the skin. Then make a cut along the underside of the front legs and front sides of the rear legs from the first cut out to each foot. Cut off the feet with game shears or a sharp knife. Gently peel the skin from each leg and off the belly. Be extra careful with the belly skin, as it tears easily. Then gently peel the skin off the hams and back up to the head. Cut off the head. Rabbits skin the easiest while the carcass is still warm.

Squirrels

If rabbits are easy to skin, squirrels more than make up for it. Squirrel skin is fairly tough, and makes a good skin for beginning tanning. Although the skin is small, it also makes good rawhide. If skinned primarily to eat, the hide is cut down the back and peeled from both ends. If the hide is to be tanned, then squirrel is skinned in the same manner as rabbit.

Groundhog

Groundhog skin is fairly thick and tough, except for the belly, and the skin makes good leather for small projects, as well as excellent rawhide. Groundhogs are normally skinned using the open method in the same manner as rabbits and squirrels.

A gambrel makes the chore easier on some animals.

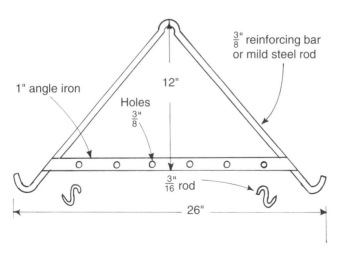

Small-game gambrel.

Common furbearers include muskrat, raccoon, opossum, beaver, otter, mink and in some areas, badger, marten and wolverine. These skins are almost always tanned with the hair on to utilize their beautiful pelts. In most instances furbearers are skinned in the cased method, although beaver is more commonly skinned in the open method and the skin stretched in the round.

Raccoon

Although one of the most popular furbearers, raccoon is also one of the toughest animals to skin. The hide sticks to the carcass like glue, particularly on older animals. You'll practically have to cut the entire hide away. And there's usually a lot of fat to be removed in the fleshing stage.

If the hide is to be frozen, or tanned immediately, you can use the open-skin method. If the hide is to be dried and stretched for future tanning, use the cased-skin method. The carcass can be skinned on a table or hung from a gambrel. I prefer the latter because the beginning cuts are best made with the legs stretched out fairly well, and this can be best accomplished with a suitable gambrel. Insert a knife point at the heel of the rear foot and slit the skin to just about an inch forward of the anus. Simply follow the hair line where the fur on the belly and the back hair joins. Repeat on the opposite leg, then join the two cuts together. Do not cut into the muscle or fat, but hold the knife blade outward to make the cuts.

At this point, make a cut encircling the ankle of each leg at the beginning of the heel cut. Work the skin off the leg, starting with the loose flap created by making the encircling cut. This can be a tough chore, especially on older, tougher-skinned animals. Wrap the flap of skin around a piece of steel rod to provide a better grip to peel the skin downward. As you pull downward, use your fingers between the skin and muscle to release the skin.

The next step is to skin out the tail. This must be done regardless of the method of storage. Make a cut on the underside of the tail and use your fingers to work the skin away from the bone, cutting carefully as you go. You can also slide a piece of stiff wire between the skin and the tailbone and slice down on one side of the wire. Be careful not to pull or cut off the end of the tail. A trapper's tail stripper (a clamp-on type plier) slides over the tailbone and helps apply pressure in removing the tailbone. A tail stripper is the best method for assuring a full tail.

The skin is then peeled down off the rest of the body to the head and front legs. Use a knife where necessary to help cut away the skin, but remember any fat and gristle left on the hide will be extremely hard to flesh away. Peel the skin down over the front legs and cut them off above the front foot. Continue to work your fingers between the skin and carcass to help peel the skin away.

Skin out the head, taking extra care not to cut through the skin and ruin the pelt. Cut around the eyes and cut through the cartilage of the ears. Cut around the lips and remove the pelt by cutting off the tip of the nose.

Muskrat

Muskrats provide a lush pelt if the animal is in its prime. Muskrats are also usually skinned in the cased method and the pelts dried on stretchers. The main difference between skinning muskrat and skinning raccoon is that the tail is first cut off before beginning the skinning process. Because the skin and meat are somewhat fragile, it's important not to pull too hard during the skinning process or you may tear the skin or the animal apart.

Other Furbearers

Mink, otter, marten, badger, weasel, skunk and possum are all skinned in the same basic method as raccoon. These critters are case skinned, using a gambrel to hold the carcass for skinning. When skinning mink and skunks, do not cut into the scent glands located on each side of the vent. Opossum are skinned in the basic same manner, except the pouch area is cut away and left on the carcass.

PREDATORS

Coyote, red and gray fox, as well as bobcat all offer luxurious furs that look great hanging on the wall, or used for clothing or accessories. Predators are also normally case skinned in the same manner as for raccoons. Begin the cuts following the line between the belly fur and back hair. It's somewhat difficult to pull the skin off the front legs so some skinners prefer to cut off the front feet be-fore hanging on the gambrel. In fact, coyote are difficult to skin; fox just a bit easier. If the skin is to be used as a wall hanging, leave the feet intact, but skin out the paws. If the skin is to be used on a garment, cut off the legs at the second joint. Again, a tail stripper makes the chore of stripping the tail much easier than by hand, or you can use a tail slitting guide.

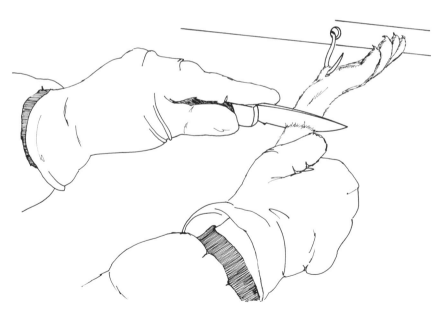

Make a cut around each ankle of the back leg.

For a cased skin, insert a knife point at the heel of the rear foot and slit the skin to the anus. Then repeat the step from the opposite foot to complete the cut.

Work the skin off of each leg, using a knife to help cut the skin away.

Carefully work the skin down over the belly and shoulders using a knife to cut the skin from the carcass where needed.

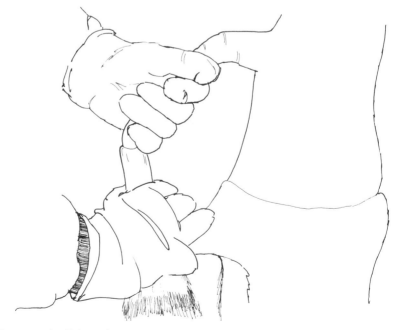

Slip or peel off the tail.

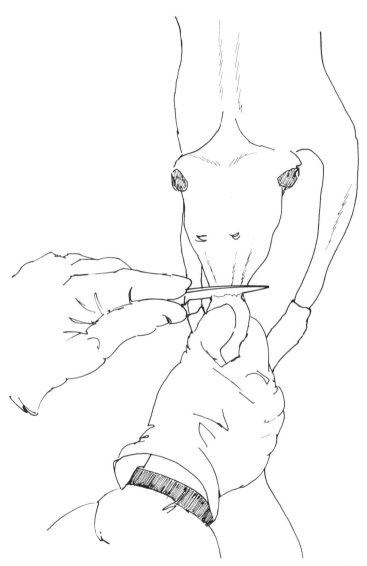

Skin out the head, taking extra care not to cut through the skin and ruin the pelt. Cut off the skin at the tip of the nose, leaving the nose tip on the pelt. Cut off the front feet.

Beaver

Even an average-sized beaver is heavy and awkward to skin. In most instances, it's easiest to skin a beaver lying belly-up on a sturdy work surface. The first step, however, is to cut off the front and rear legs. The easiest way to do this is to use a small hand hatchet and a chopping block. Then cut off the tail by first cutting through the skin and muscle at the base of the tail with a sharp knife, then again using the hatchet and chopping block to chop off the tail.

With the beaver lying belly-up, and starting at the cutoff tail area, make a cut through the belly skin all the way to the tip of the chin. Make sure you do not cut into the belly muscle. Very carefully peel the belly skin back, using a sharp, rounded-point skinning knife to assist in cutting the skin away from the muscle. Beaver pelts are extremely valuable. Make sure you don't cut through the skin or into the intestines, which can spill matter over the valuable pelt. Also, do not cut into the castor glands located just ahead of the vent. As you skin the belly, pull the hide down and around the sides until it is lying flat on both sides of the carcass. Once the belly and sides have been skinned, turn the carcass over and skin out the back. Carefully skin out the head. Cut around the eyes and ears and finally cut through the nose to remove the pelt.

Beaver has a lot of gristle and fat, and it's important to skin the critter as carefully as possible, using a good skinning knife to work the hide off the flesh. Keep as much fat off the skin as possible.

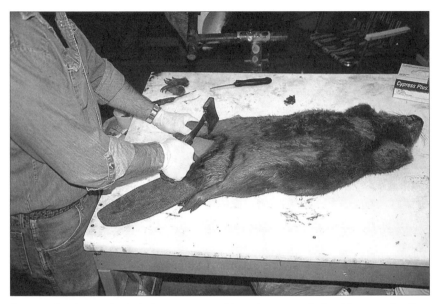

Some animals, particularly beavers, are skinned open pelt. In this case the first step is to cut off the feet.

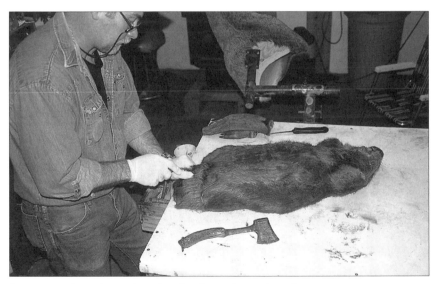

Starting at the tail cut, slice the skin from the underside.

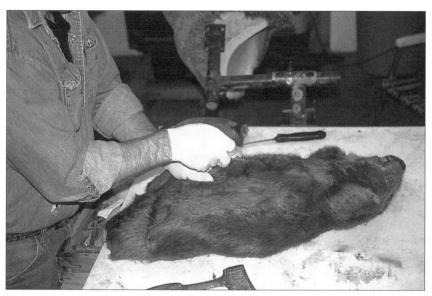

Work the cut all the way up the belly, being careful not to cut into the belly muscle.

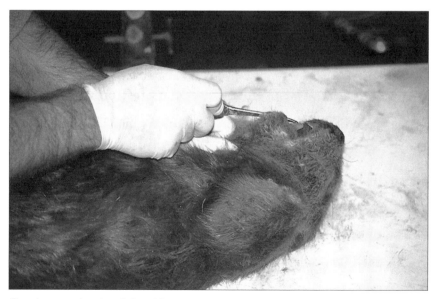

Continue to the tip of the chin.

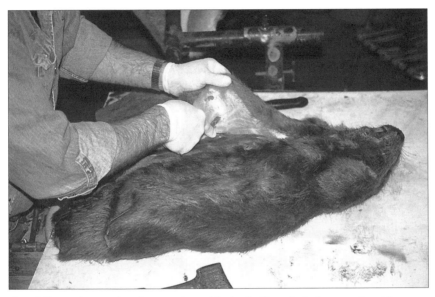

Carefully peel away the skin, cutting with the knife to help loosen the skin.

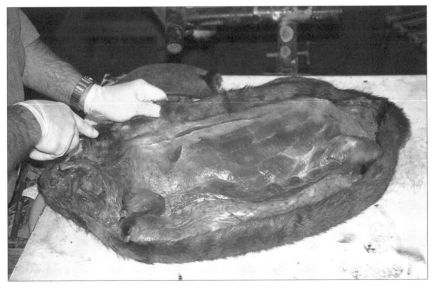

Make sure you don't cut through the skin—take your time.

Once the belly side is finished, turn the animal over and work on its back.

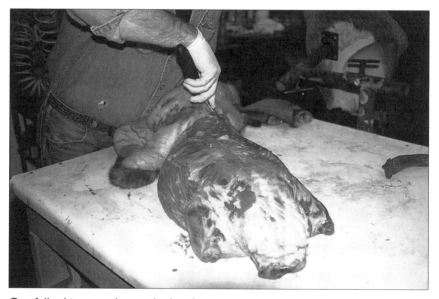

Carefully skin up and over the head.

The finished pelt and the carcass.

CHAPTER 5

Skinning Deer, Big Game and Domestic Animals

P roperly skinning deer, big game, bear and domestic animals is extremely important in order to end up with a nice pelt, rug or leather product. The animal should be skinned as soon as possible and the hide properly preserved until it can be tanned.

DEER AND BIG GAME ANIMALS

Skinning deer and medium-sized game is easiest with the animal hanging head-down from a gambrel. Bear and the brutes such as moose and elk are usually skinned on the ground, unless a method is available to transport the carcass quickly to a campsite skinning pole. In this case, the critter may be field dressed and skinned later.

Following is basic information on skinning deer while hanging. Elk, moose, caribou, antelope, sheep and goats can all be skinned in this method. This method is used for nontrophy animals that won't be used for a full head mount. Trophy heads to be mounted are skinned following the caping information later in this chapter. Caping will cut the skin basically in half, but even half a skin can be tanned for use in leather projects. It's a shame to waste any usable portion of the animal.

First step is to cut off the rear legs just below the hocks. Insert the point of a knife blade from the side opposite the scent glands in the hock area and make a cut between the bone and tendon. Do this for each rear leg to create an opening for the gambrel. Insert the gambrel in place, and hoist up the carcass. I like to hoist only high enough to easily reach the rear legs and ham area at this time, then raise the animal as I work down. Starting at the inside of one ham, make a slit in the skin up to just about the hock area containing the gambrel point. Cut around

First step in skinning deer and big game is to cut off the rear legs below the hocks and cut the front legs off above the knee.

Most big game is skinned the easiest hanging from a gambrel.

the leg at this point, leaving skin in the hock and gambrel-point area. This portion of the leg contains almost no meat and is cut away during the butchering process.

Make the initial skinning cuts downward from outside the skin; then, during all other skinning cuts, keep the knife blade pointed outward to avoid cutting down through the hair. Cut from the underside of the skin, with the knife blade facing outward. This prevents cutting hairs that can detract from the quality of the hide that is to be tanned with the hair on. And it prevents getting cut hairs on the meat.

At this point I take a shortcut. I raise the animal and cut off the front legs just behind the knee joint. Make a cut in the skin on the inside of the legs from the cutoff

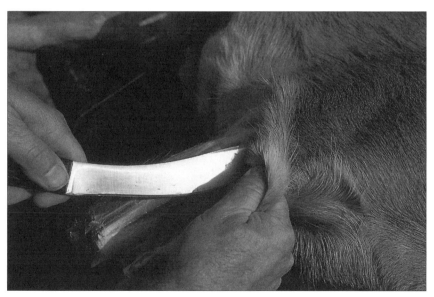

To make skinning easier, skin out the front legs first.

legs to the center of the chest. Skin out the front legs to the shoulders. There's a reason for this step. As the hide is peeled off, it tends to drape down over the front legs, making skinning them at that time a chore. If the front legs are done first, it makes the whole process of skinning much easier.

Then go back up to the rear of the carcass and skin around the inside of the ham and the leg, using the knife blade between the inside of the skin and the meat to help remove the skin. Cut and pull at the same time. Do both hams down to the tail by cutting and pulling the skin.

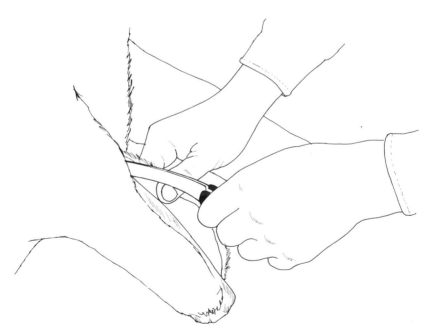

Make a cut from the cutoff leg with the knife blade facing up, along the back side of the leg.

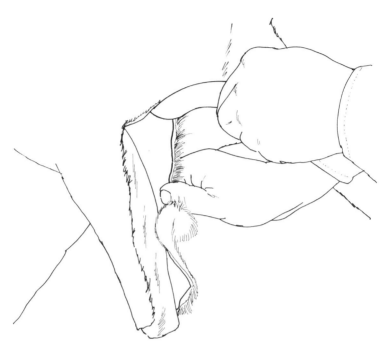

Continue the cut across the chest to the cut at the end of the breastbone or throat.

Skin around the base of the tail to expose the bone, then cut off the tail with a meat saw or hand saw.

Move back up to the ham area and continue to cut and pull the hide down. Once you get the hide started on the sides and back, it can often be "fisted" or pulled down and away fairly easily. Use the knife to release the hide from the meat as needed. Try to leave as much meat and fat on the carcass and off the skin as possible. This will make fleshing the hide much easier.

Once the skin drapes down around the shoulders and front legs, continue to cut and pull the skin away from

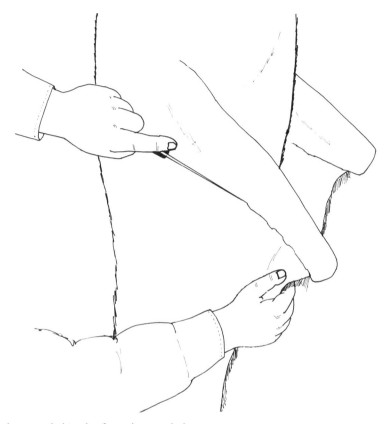

Peel out and skin the front legs and chest area.

the area. Continue pulling and cutting the skin, allowing it to drape down as you go to the base of the neck. Continue hoisting the carcass higher as you work in order to make the work easier without having to stoop or bend over. As with skinning any animal for the hide or pelt, make sure you don't cut through the skin and create holes. You can quickly ruin a hide. Use a sharp skinning knife with a rounded point and keep it sharp.

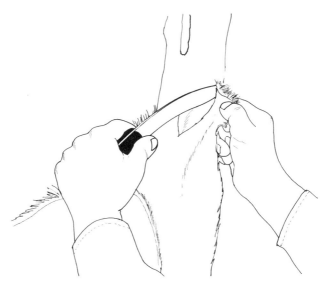

Then go back up to the rear legs and, with the skinning knife blade pointed out, make a cut in the skin just below the hocks.

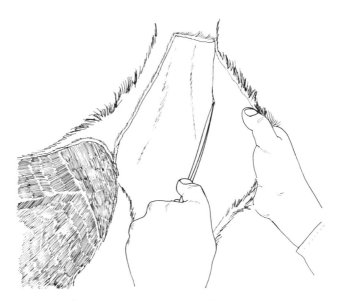

Peel the skin away from the leg and inside of the ham, using a sharp skinning knife to cut away stubborn areas.

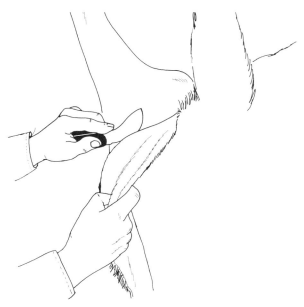

Work around the leg and ham, pulling the hide and cutting with the knife to release as needed.

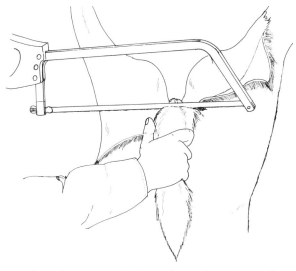

Once down to the tail, cut through the tailbone from the underside, leaving the tail on the skin.

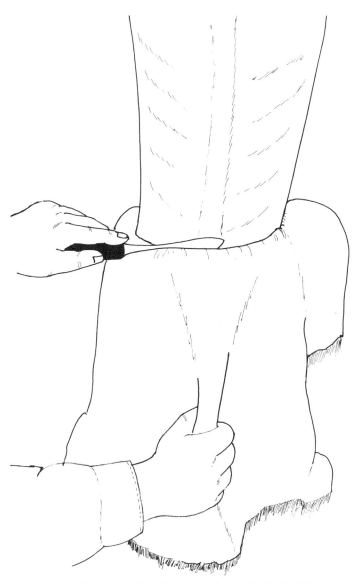

Continue peeling and cutting the skin away from the back, belly and sides. In many instances the skin will pull away quite easily until you get to the shoulder area.

Skin down to the head and cut the head off.

Cut the head off. This can be done with a sharp knife, slicing around the head and neck joint at the junction of the jaw and neck. Then twist the head to release the bone connection. After the bone releases, cut the remaining muscles holding the head in place.

The hide should immediately be preserved in some manner, especially if you intend to tan it with the hair on. The chapter on preserving and storing hides and skins explains the details of preserving if the hide won't be tanned immediately after skinning.

Caping

The head of a trophy deer or other big game animal suitable for mounting must be caped before skinning. The caping method takes almost half the hide; however, a half hide can be used for many leather projects, including for rawhide.

The first step toward proper caping begins in the field dressing. Do not cut the skin at the throat or split the breastbone while the skin is on the carcass. Cut around the cape first. Most hunters don't leave enough of the skin for a proper mount, thinking that only the neck in front of the shoulders is enough. The best tactic is to cut the cape starting behind the front shoulders and at the rear of the withers on the back of the animal. The first cut is from the withers, behind the front shoulders and down to the belly on each side, meeting at the breastbone.

Then cut down the inside of the front legs to just above the front joint. Make a circle cut around the legs. The next cut starts at the top of the withers and proceeds to the back of the skull behind the antlers, approximately between the ears. Part the hair, and make this cut as straight and smooth as possible. It's a good idea to make the cut from the inside to prevent cutting through the hairs on the top of the neck. This makes a better seam when sewn together by the taxidermist. Make sure you stop the cut before you get between the antlers. Then make a Y cut from the neck up to the rear of each antler base.

Pull the cape off, starting behind the shoulders and using the knife to loosen as needed. When you get to the joint of the neck and skull, remove the head. Pull the skin well forward of the area to be cut, and keep the skin

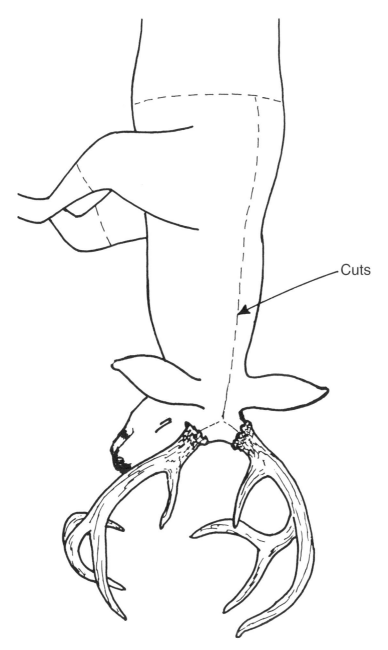

Cuts

Dotted lines show the skinning cuts needed for caping a head for mounting.

out of the way so you don't accidentally cut it in severing the head from the carcass. Cut through the muscle over the large neck joint just behind the skull. Cut around the neck at this point. Bend the head back so you can expose the muscle and sinew that needs to be cut. Once all have been cut, the head will twist off. Immediately salt the exposed head and skin. Most taxidermists prefer the cape to be delivered in this manner; however, this can only be done in cool weather. Remember to salt in the eyes, ears and nostril openings as well. This is all that needs to be done if the cape is to be taken to the taxidermist within a few days. If you can't get the cape to the taxidermist immediately, you may wish to freeze the entire "package."

BEAR

Because bear skins are fairly thick, and with the heavy fur and the amount of fat under the skin, the skin can begin to deteriorate very quickly, especially in warm or hot weather. Skin the critter as quickly as possible.

If the skinning is to be a shoulder wall mount rather than utilized as a rug, you should field dress and cape the head and shoulders in the same method as described for other big game. Make sure you don't cut too far up the throat and belly to ruin the skin of the head and shoulders for a good wall mount.

In most instances, however, a bear skin is used as a rug, or in some cases as a full mount. In this case the carcass is skinned somewhat differently than for the antlered or horned game. If the bear is a possible trophy, you should first measure the carcass from the tip of the nose to the tip of the tail and from outstretched foot to outstretched foot. If a rug is to be made, measure the length and circumference of the head. Finally, measure the length of the tail.

The first skinning cuts are actually made during the field-dressing steps. The first step is to put on disposable latex gloves, then roll the animal over on its back on a flat, smooth surface. If possible, position the head slightly higher than the rest of the body.

Make a shallow, 2- to 3-inch cut to one side of the penis if a male. Gently cut through the skin, but not the inner intestine lining. You may wish to remove the penis and scrotum of a male at this time if allowed by law. (Check local laws. Some states require the genitals to remain on the field-dressed carcass until the animal has been checked at a field station.) This cut should run from the anal vent to the chin. The cut to the chin can either be to the bottom of the center of the chin, or angled off to one side of the mouth. The latter is preferred for bear rugs, as the sewn seam won't show as much. Do not, however, cut into the lips.

The carcass is then field dressed and the skinning continued. A second cut is made from the pad of one hind foot, along the inside of the thin skin of the inner hind leg, to the base of the tail. The cut then continues along the opposite leg to the pad on the opposite foot.

The third cut is made in the same manner on the thin inside skin of the front legs. The hide is then peeled

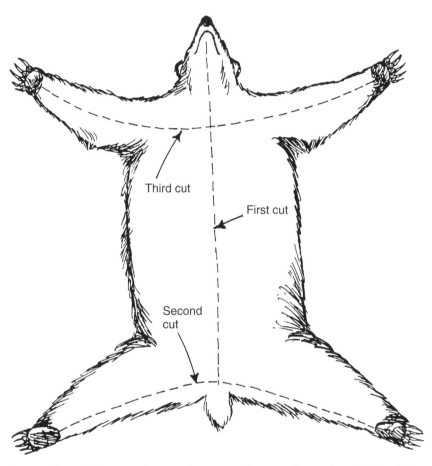

Because bear skins are often used as rugs, they are dressed and skinned in a somewhat different matter. The initial cuts for skinning a bear.

away from the carcass, beginning on the hind end and working toward the head. Roll and position the carcass in order to loosen all the skin, yet keep the meat on the skin to prevent getting dirt and debris into it. A tarp or other cover for the ground can also help protect the meat during the skinning process as well as keep dirt and debris from the hair.

When you reach the joint of the skull and neck, cut through the muscle and tissue at the joint, then twist the head until it comes free. Cut away any remaining tissue.

Although some hunters merely cut off the feet and leave the feet and claws with the hide, the best method is to skin out the pads and feet. This prevents any possible deterioration of the feet and claws. Cut around all four foot pads to skin them out, but leave the toe pads.

A bear skin has a lot of fat, and it's extremely important to remove all fat and tissue from the hide. The easiest way to remove the fat is to do so as you skin the bear. The longer you work on the hide, the harder it becomes to remove the fat and underlying tissue.

DOMESTIC ANIMALS

Goats and sheep provide excellent leather products, but must also be skinned properly. They are normally suspended from gambrels and skinned in much the same manner as deer. Both are fairly easy to skin, especially if skinned while the carcass is still warm.

Make a cut from the anal vent to the tip of the chin. Make sure you keep the sheep wool separated from the meat so you don't contaminate it as you make the cut. Cut around the front legs at the first joint and then cut from the leg cuts up to the first cut. Cut through the skin around each hock of the rear leg, then cut through the skin on the inside of the leg to the first cut near the anal vent. Beginning at the hock cut, peel the skin away and down over the hams. Again, keep the wool from touching the meat. "Fist" the hide down as you go. It will peel off fairly easily. The easiest method is to cut off the skin at the base of the skull, as the head skin is rarely used. You can, however, skin out the entire head, cutting around ears, eyes and lips.

Goats are skinned in the same manner, except they're a bit harder to skin because the ligaments tend to stick to the skin. Use your fingers and hands to "fist" off the hide as you work it downward.

Pigs are hard to skin, primarily because there isn't much delineation between skin and fat, so the skin tends to hold a lot of fat. The skin, especially on the back of larger animals, is also quite thick. Pig skin is also somewhat hard to tan. For these reasons, in the old days most farm-butchered pigs were scalded and scraped. Modern-day butchers, who do not utilize the skin, make cuts lengthwise of the carcass and peel and cut off the skin in strips. To skin, hang by gambrels and make the traditional cuts in the belly and legs. Then use a knife to cut the skin away from the fat. Keep as much fat as possible off the skin, as it is hard to flesh off.

Calf skin is a very valuable product, and calves are fairly easy to skin. They are skinned in the same manner as described for sheep and goats.

Mature cattle, especially larger cows, steers and bulls, are not particularly hard to skin. They are normally skinned while hanging, and it does require sturdy equipment to hoist and hold them in place for skinning. Mature cattle are skinned using the same basic cuts as for big

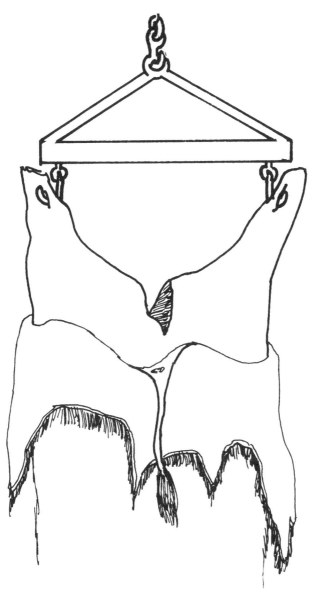

Large game and domestic animals such as cattle are skinned hung head-down from sturdy gambrels.

game. The biggest problem is that large cow and bull hides are quite heavy, not only during the skinning process, but during the tanning as well. You may wish to cut the hide in half for easier working. Use the same basic cuts to start off the skinning, then use a knife to help cut the skin away from the carcass. In most operations for commercial tanning, the head is skinned, but the home tanner will probably prefer to simply cut the skin off around the neck at the back of the skull.

Horses and buffalo are skinned in the same basic manner. Again, it requires not a little equipment and hard work.

CHAPTER

6

Preserving and Storing Hides and Pelts

The best way to tan a hide or pelt is to begin the process as soon as the skin comes off the animal. For most of us, however, that's rarely possible. For one thing, it's usually easier to tan more than one hide at a time. Doing several hides with each step takes just a little more time than doing one hide. And often we just don't have time at the moment to stop and tan a hide. The weather and timing of the year can also have an effect. Tanning is hard work, and doing many of the chores in the summer months can be extremely hot.

So for the most part, hides must be preserved and stored until they can be tanned. Several methods of storing can be used, including drying and stretching, salting, freezing and/or a combination of these methods. Regardless of the methods chosen, it's important to start the preserving process as soon after the animal has been killed as possible. Decay of the natural materials in the hide begins immediately after death, and this breakdown process must be stopped to produce a quality hide or fur. If you're in deer camp, or the elk mountains, the weather is hot and you

Hides and pelts must be properly preserved until they can be tanned.

don't have access to a freezer, the first step is to immediately flesh and salt the hide. Each step, regardless of whether small game, furbearer pelt or big game hide, is extremely important, although somewhat different steps are required for the different hides and pelts. Furbearers are usually fleshed and air dried.

Preserving Furs

The fur or hair-on skins from small game, furbearers and predators is normally preserved simply by drying as these pelts are often collected over a season and then sold to fur buyers. The quality of the pelt is directly related to the amount of effort put into skinning and then fleshing and proper stretching.

The chapter on skinning illustrates the techniques on skinning the different animals. The next step is proper fleshing—and I can't stress this step enough.

Fleshing

Removing all flesh, meat and fat in the hypodermis layer on the underside of the skin is the first and foremost step in a quality tanned pelt or hide. If all the materials are not removed, the skin or hide will not tan properly, and on pelts this means the fur could fall out after the hide has been tanned. Some furbearers and predators are fairly hard to flesh, but it must be done. Take your time and make sure all materials are removed. You can freeze the hide and then do the fleshing at a more convenient time, but I've found by the time the hide thaws thoroughly you may

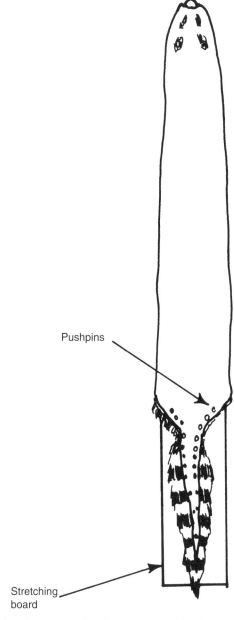

Pushpins

Stretching
board

One method with pelts is to air dry them on stretching frames or boards.

already be standing a chance of losing some hair. And in some instances the fat and membrane layer sticks to the hide much more after freezing than if the chore is done while the hide is still warm. If the hide is left in the freezer too long, the fat and membrane can also freezer burn to the skin, making them almost impossible to remove.

Properly fleshing furbearers and predators is also somewhat more difficult than with hair-off hides for leather. Pelts are made up of several layers: the hair or fur, the skin layers and the fat layer. If you flesh too deeply into the skin in an attempt to remove the fat layer, you can cut the hair roots on the inner side of the skin, again resulting in fur falling out. But if you don't get the fat layer off, the tanning materials can't penetrate properly and the result is again a poor tanning job. Determining the starting and stopping point between the layer of fat and the innermost surface of the skin takes some practice. You'll probably make a few mistakes at first, but will soon learn to recognize the smooth, inner surface of the skin after the fat layer has been removed. Removing the fat layer from some animals, such as beaver, raccoon and coyote, is not a simple chore and in some areas requires not a little pressure. Unfortunately, it's also easy to cut right through the skin and rip or tear it as well. There's often a fine line in the amount of pressure needed or that can be used in fleshing.

The tools for fleshing are simple. A fleshing beam fitted to the size of the animal is important. You can use an all-around-sized beam for open-skinned animals, but one more fitted to smaller skins is important for cased skins. The beam end should be about stomach height of the person doing the fleshing.

The flesh can be removed with several items, including a skinning knife or draw knife. A curved fleshing knife is the best choice, and I prefer one with one side flat or dull and one side sharp. The dull side can be used for most work, but the really tough spots, such as around the neck and hips, normally require a sharp blade. A knife sharpener, rubber gloves, waterproof apron and a bucket to catch the scrapings are also required. A large piece of cardboard placed under the fleshing beam, especially if fleshing inside, will help catch the drippings and eliminate most of the mess.

Before you start fleshing, examine the fur for any hard objects, such as burrs, dirt clods, even small rocks. Comb

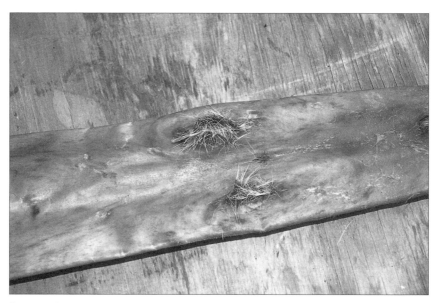

Some pelts are dried fur-side in, some fur-side out. The skin will dry to a hard surface.

In all instances it is important to completely split the tail if it is to be left on the hide.

Regardless of the method used for preserving, the hide must first be fleshed. All meat, fat and inner membrane must be removed using a fleshing knife.

or brush the fur smooth. Even though the fleshing knife is used on the opposite or inside of the skin, it can catch on the bump caused by the obstacle and cause a tear in the skin.

With the flesh side out, slip the cased skin over the fleshing beam until the nose of the animal hits the end. With some animals the skin can tear easily, so use your belly to add pressure to help hold the skin in place. Then, beginning with the dull side of the fleshing knife, hold the knife with the blade edge turned toward you and use a pushing motion to scrape or "flesh" the materials away. If the dull side doesn't catch in the fat layer, turn to the sharp side to begin the strokes, then turn back to the dull side to continue pushing the fat layer away. Vary the pressure as needed to cut down through the fat layer to the underskin layer. In most instances, you should start just behind the ears with the scraper. The head and nose area are almost impossible to flesh with the scraper. A rounded-point skinning knife or pelt scraper does the best job in these areas. My favorite technique is to start at the top of the skin, just behind the ears, and scrape downward. The skin tends to stretch during this process, and as it becomes a longer reach with the fleshing knife, I simply turn the skin on the fleshing beam and continue to flesh the forward portion. Once I have that area fleshed, I then pull the skin up over the board to reach new areas and again turn the skin as needed. Hold the skin in place with your belly against the fleshing beam as you scrape.

On some animals you'll start to gather a pretty good amount of fat and flesh as you go, and it's tempting to cut this off with a sharp knife. I do cut it off, but it's important to keep the "rolled-up" edge "working." Once you get the layer started, it tends to keep rolling with the pressure. If the edge is removed, you have to dig in with the fleshing knife to restart the process. So cut off the excess, but keep the rolled edge in place. When you reach the edge of the hide the fat layer tends to stick in place. Using the fleshing knife across the beam to cut off this material dulls the knife. When I reach that point, I cut off the waste with a sharp knife.

Don't get lazy and flesh down on the sides of the fleshing beam. Fleshing down the sides of the fleshing beam is a good way to cut the hide. Instead, keep turning the hide and flesh only on the top of the beam.

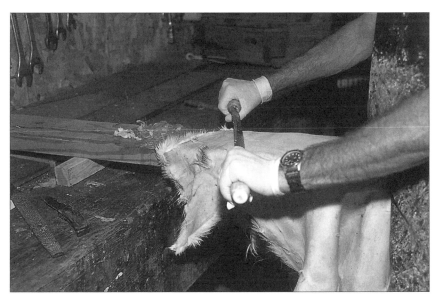

Drape the hide over a fleshing beam, holding it in place with your belly; the fleshing knife is used with push strokes to roll the materials off the hide.

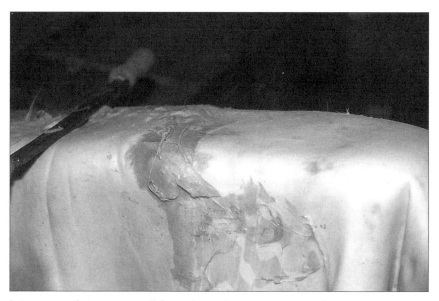

It is extremely important all fat and membrane are removed.

If the skin will be used as a wall hanging, rug or hat, leave the ears and nose attached, but cut off the bottom lips to "square off" the jaw line and make a smoother-looking head. If keeping the skin intact, skin out the ears, reversing them as needed.

On some cased animals the front legs are left as holes, and these can present problems. The flaps of skin want to twist and turn with the pressure from the fleshing knife, and the skin can easily tear. One method is to push these areas over the small end of the fleshing beam.

Be very careful on the belly that you don't slice through the teats on the underside of female animals. It happens easily and can cause a bad tear in the pelt.

The tail should have been split during the skinning process. If it hasn't, split the tail with a sharp knife, tail stripper or rod run alongside the bone to lift the skin for slitting. Then thoroughly flesh the underside of the spread-out tail skin.

Make sure you get all the fat layer off the skin around the base of the tail area and over the hips. Fleshing to the end of the tail makes for a supple and long-lasting tail. When fleshing the back legs, lay them out flat on the fleshing beam and make sure you get them cleaned thoroughly.

Once all materials have been removed from the skin, hang it up by the nose. Use a clean, dry cloth to clean the skin and wipe off all loosened grease and liquid.

Uncased Skin

An uncased or open-skinned pelt is fleshed in the same manner. Open-skinned pelts are actually easier to do because the skin is opened up and can be spread out easily on the beam. They will, however, have a tendency to slip sideways as you flesh on the edges and are a bit harder to hold in place with your belly. If the pelt will be used for clothing, cut off the head where the neck joins. Fleshing and tanning the head, ears and nose requires extra effort. Again, make sure all materials are removed from the back of the skin, with the skin lying on the beam, wipe with a dry cloth.

Stretching

Raw fur sold to fur buyers is usually dried on stretchers. Stretching is also a fairly easy way to store a number of pelts until you can tan them. Stretchers are available either of metal or of wood and are sized to fit the various species. It's important to match the stretcher size to the animal.

The techniques for drying are somewhat different with the different stretchers.

Metal stretchers are made of a springy wire. They are compressed and the pelt slid over the wire frame. When dry, the metal stretchers are again compressed and the dried pelt removed. In most instances the pelt is stretched with the fur inside, or semi-dried and the skin turned right side out. Stretchers are made to fit the pelts fairly snugly, and it may take some effort with some animals to get the pelt in place. But be patient and carefully work the pelt in place. Make sure the pelt is centered on the stretcher, and pull the pelt down until the animal's head fits snugly on the top end of the stretcher. The stretchers have sliding metal arms with hooks on them. The hooks of one arm are fastened through the skin at the base of the tail, about ½ inch from the edge. The teeth of the second arm are used to hold the bottom of the back feet. Once the teeth are fastened securely in the skin, pull the arms down to tighten and stretch the skin.

Pelts have traditionally been stretched on wooden stretchers, and you can make your own stretchers fairly economically from pine shelving materials. Again, it's important that the stretcher match the size of the animal. The dimensions have become fairly standard because fur buyers demand specific sizes. Shown in Chapter 2 are the most common sizes. Cut the boards to shape, round their edges with a draw knife, then sand smooth. A tapered wooden wedge is used with the stretcher to stretch the pelt on the form.

The pelt is pulled down over the stretcher board in the same manner, making sure it is centered and aligned properly. Pushpins are pressed into the board to hold the pelt in place. A pin is used on either side of the base of the tail and one in each hind leg, pulling the pelt down evenly and taut.

Wood stretchers also offer an advantage in that the tail can be spread out and pinned in placed as well. Once the pelt has been thoroughly pinned in place, the wooden wedge is inserted in the belly side and pushed up in place with the tip into the nose area to further stretch the pelt. Skin shrinks as it dries, and will become quite tight on the stretcher. Removing the wooden wedge allows space to pull the skin off the stretcher.

Before placing the pelts on the stretcher, make sure the fur side is not soaking wet. This can cause drying problems, especially on wood stretchers.

Drying

Once the pelts have been placed on the stretcher, they must be properly dried. Raw fur sold to buyers is simply dried with no salt or other preservatives added. The same method can be used for furs you wish to tan yourself. Furs will dry fairly easily at temperatures above 40 degrees F. Do not allow the pelts to freeze and, if possible, avoid temperatures over 60 degrees. Drying will usually take from two to three days to a little over a week, depending on the temperature and humidity. Wire stretchers are normally hung by hooks with the nose end up. Wood stretchers can have a hole drilled in

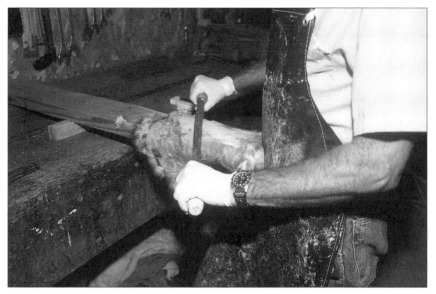

Some hides, particularly some of the furbearers, are extremely hard to flesh. Take your time and be patient.

their base and hung upside down from a hook. The best place to dry is from the rafters of a building that has good air circulation.

Once the pelts are dried, they can be left on the stretchers until you're ready to tan. Or they can be slipped off the stretchers and stored in a cool, dry place. The pelts should be protected from mice, rats, squirrels and other rodents. Again, a good method is to suspend them from a rafter or ceiling. Don't, however, use rope or heavy string that mice can climb down. Instead use a wire loop. Pelts stored in this manner will usually suffer no damage for several months during cool or cold weather. In hot weather, however, insect damage can occur. If pelts must be keep through the hot months, they should be in a freezer. Wrap the pelt tightly with freezer paper and place in a plastic bag to help ensure against freezer burn.

Open-Skinned Small Game

Small game and furbearer hides are also sometimes skinned by the open method. In the old days the hides were fleshed and then simply nailed to the inside of the barn door. That method still works for drying and cool-weather storage. Stretch the hide out as taut as possible without tearing and use roofing nails to tack the hide in place. If you don't have a convenient barn door, a sheet of plywood will work.

Make sure to clean the oils and fat from your fleshing beam after each use.

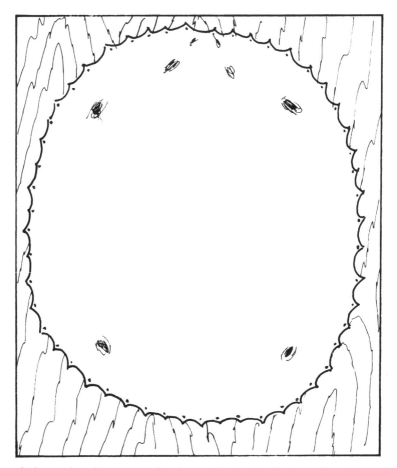

Some hides, such as beaver, are dried stretched and tacked to a board.

Beaver is commonly skinned by the open method and is also stretched in this manner. No. 8 common nails should be used instead of roofing nails. Once the skin begins to shrink and becomes tight on the nails, pull the hide up off the wood surface to the tops of the nails. This provides more air circulation to dry the thick pelt.

Freezing

Small game skins can also be frozen for future use. Just make sure they are completely fleshed first. Then fold flesh sides together and roll tight. Place the skin in a plastic bag and tie shut. Mark the contents. You don't want to open a coyote skin package instead of a rump roast for Sunday dinner.

DEER AND OTHER BIG GAME

As with small game, larger hides can also be air dried or frozen. Proper fleshing is just as important on the larger

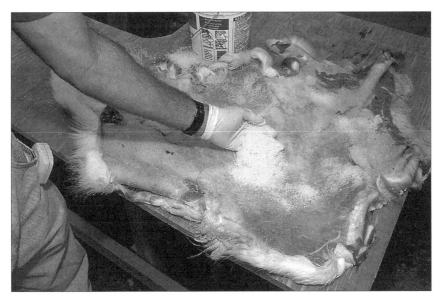

Some hides are preserved by salting and stored dry or frozen. A pound of salt per pound of hide is normally used.

animal hides. In some instances, especially of white-tailed deer, fleshing is actually easier than on some of the furbearers. On larger hides, such as elk or moose, the biggest problem is the weight of the hide. You may wish to cut the hide into two pieces, down the center of the back. This makes it easier to handle not only while fleshing, but throughout the tanning process.

Fleshing is necessary for air drying and is best even when the hides are to be frozen. Fleshing is much, much easier before the hides freeze.

The different layers of the skin are somewhat easier to discern on the larger skins. Be sure to get all the innermost fat and membrane completely off the skin. Examine the skin in good light to make sure you haven't left any small areas of fat or membrane. The same curved fleshing knife is used, and in the case of larger skins you can usually use the sharp side for most of the skin, except the belly area and on the legs. It's easier to cut through the skin in these areas.

A large, rounded fleshing beam is best for the larger animals, as it's easier to cover more area with the fleshing knife and the hide tends to stay in place easier than on a small beam. On large hides I prefer to start fleshing strokes in the center of the hide and work toward the outside edges. This allows you to turn the hide as you work yet keep the hide well centered so it doesn't slide off the beam. As you accumulate large amounts of fat and membrane, cut off the excess, but again leave the working edge for the knife to catch. Sometimes it's hard to get the membrane to turn loose at the edges of the hide, and this can be cut off with a sharp knife as well. Be extra careful around holes, as the knife can catch and tear the

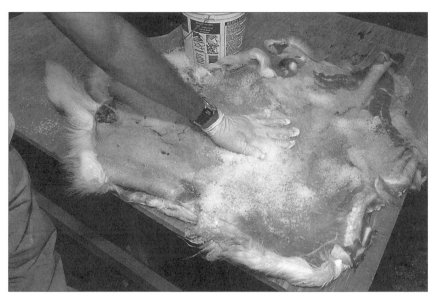

Make sure the salt is well rubbed into all surfaces.

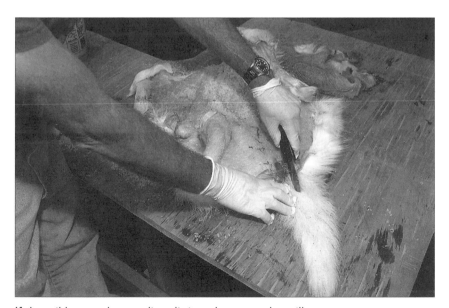

If the tail has not been split, split it and remove the tailbone.

hide. Unless the hide is to be used as a wall mount or rug, cut off the tail and trim the edges of all ragged portions.

Air Drying

Large game hides can be air dried, but first they must be salted. The first step is to weigh the hide. Then spread the hide out on a flat, smooth surface and make sure all wrinkles are out, especially around the edges and along the leg areas. Pour a generous amount of salt onto the hide. Ordinary stock salt works well and is inexpensive. Use at least a pound of salt per pound of hide. Wearing latex gloves, rub the salt over all portions of the hide, paying particular attention to the edges, around the legs and the tail area. The neck area of moose, large elk and other animals is often ½ inch or more thick, and salt will not penetrate fully in these areas. Score these areas with shallow, crisscrossing cuts, then apply the salt. Make sure each and every portion of the hide is well covered with salt. Then fold the hide, flesh-side in. Roll the hide up and place it on a sloping surface, away from pets and where other critters can't get to it. In a couple of days, unroll, shake out the old salt and apply new salt and roll. Allow the hide to sit for a couple more days, then spread it out to dry. You can also tack the hide to the traditional inside of a barn door, or a piece of plywood, to prevent it from curling during the drying process. Protect the hide from moisture and pests.

Deer and other big game hides can also be frozen. One winter I had seven such hides in my freezer. Believe me, they took up a lot of space. Again, the hides should

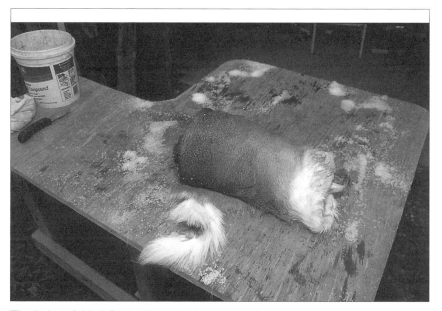

The hide is folded, flesh sides together, then rolled up.

Leave hide overnight, open up and reapply salt. The hide must be put someplace where it will drain well. Large cowhides are left folded flat.

be well fleshed before freezing. Roll up the fleshed hides, flesh sides folded together before rolling, and place in plastic bags. Tie the bags shut and label. I've also frozen fleshed and dehaired deer skins, and they take up a lot less room.

Tanning Small Game and Furbearers

Before tanning any hides or skins, the first step is to determine what the skin will be used for. Small game and furbearer skins make great-looking wall hangings or throw rugs. The pelts can also be used with the fur on for garments. Or in some instances, you may wish to dehair and make leather from some small game skins.

Fur-On Tanning

If the skin has been fleshed and frozen, the tanning process goes fairly quickly. Simply thaw the skin. But do not allow the skin to sit for a long period of time or the skins will deteriorate and the hair will start to slip and fall out.

If the skin has been cured or dried, soak it in several changes of cool water in a plastic tub. Again, do not allow the skin to sit very long, as the hair will begin to slip. Continually check for the stiffness of the hide and remove as soon as the hide begins to become flexible

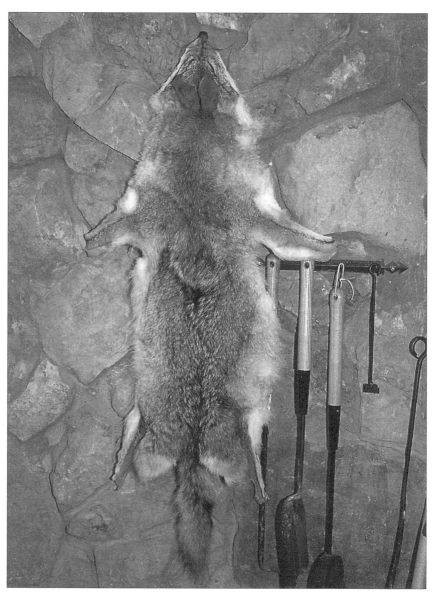

Small game and furbearers are fairly easily tanned. They can be tanned into wall hangings or rugs.

enough to work. This will usually take only two to three hours, depending on the air or room temperature. Adding borax to the water, 1 ounce to each gallon of water, plus a bit of dish soap helps clean the skin, cuts the grease and helps to relax it. Then rinse in clean water. Incidentally, only soft water should be used during the tanning processes, as the lime in some hard waters can deter the processes.

Extremely greasy skins, such as beaver or raccoon, should first be degreased. Small skins can be soaked in naphtha or white gas. Large skins are degreased by sprinkling the degreaser onto both the flesh and hair side; then sprinkle sawdust over both surfaces and work the sawdust into the surfaces. The sawdust absorbs the grease and degreaser. Make sure you do this chore outside or in a well-ventilated area with no open flames or pilot lights; as easier method of degreasing is with Rittel's Degreaser.

Hang the degreased skins outside to allow them to dry and use a small stick or kitchen spatula to beat the sawdust out of the skins. The furs should be fluffed at this time. Sprinkle borax over the furs, then use a stick or spatula to beat out the materials. Once all materials are removed from the skins, rinse them in clean, cool water and squeeze the skin to remove excess water and partially dry it.

Several different tanning methods can be used for small game and furbearers. Turpentine and alcohol is a good method for very small game such as rabbits or squirrels, and it's a good learning technique. Salt and alum tannage is one of the least expensive methods and easy for a beginner as well. Skins tanned in this method

Furbearers and small game can also be tanned hair-on for garments or dehaired for very fine leather.

do tend to be fairly stiff and hard to soften, but it is a traditional method with fur-on tanning of such animals as coyotes and raccoons. Acid tans are commonly used on small game as well. Chrome tannage produces one of the most durable products, but is more difficult to do and turns the skin blue. Glutaraldehyde tannage produces extremely good-quality skins, but the materials are more costly and somewhat harder to obtain. The latter two methods are used less commonly for fur-on tanning. Tanning fur-on small game is also very easy using one of the tanning oil agents available. This is also one of the simplest methods.

Turpentine and Alcohol

Pour equal parts alcohol and turpentine into a large-mouthed gallon jar with a plastic screw top. There should be enough liquid in the jar to cover the skin; about a pint of each will usually suffice. Place the skin in the jar and shake or stir the solution several times each day for 7 to 10 days. Remove the skin and wash it thoroughly in water to which dishwashing or laundry detergent has been added. Rinse the skin in clean water, changing the water a number of times to make sure all the detergent is removed.

Squeeze the skin to partially dry it. Then apply a finishing oil to the flesh side of the skin. A bit of neat's-foot oil is excellent. Don't, however, overdo it. Apply just enough to lightly oil the skin.

Work the skin over a fleshing beam, or a breaking stake, or work by stretching and pulling the skin to soften. This must be done over a period of time as the skin dries, but before the skin dries completely. On a small skin, this process may take only a day. The actual stretching motion consists of grasping the skin in both hands and working it over the edge of an object, much like shining your shoes. I like to keep the skin hanging over the stake and go about other chores, continually coming back and stretching a bit, letting my shoulders rest and then working again. Other means of stretching include working through smooth metal rings or even over a chair back or a board clamped in a vise. Regardless, there should be no sharp edges on the stretching object to catch and tear the skin. To produce a soft, supple skin requires repeated stretching; it's quite a bit of work, even on a small skin.

Rittel's EZ-100 Rabbit Skin Tanning Method

This is a particularly easy technique and great for learning how to tan. Rittel's EZ-100 tanning agent is safe to use, environmentally friendly and produces a soft, white-leather tanned skin that you can even wash. The quantity of solutions to be made up will tan 8 to 12 full-sized rabbit skins.

The skins should first be well fleshed. Work from the tail toward the head when fleshing these delicate skins, as they tear easily. If the skin has been dried or frozen,

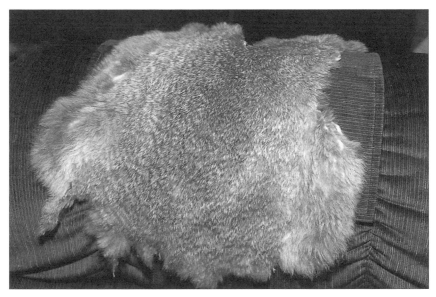

Domestic or wild rabbit skins are great for learning how to tan.

The skin should have been properly fleshed and preserved. Quite often small game is stretched and air dried.

soak it in a relaxing bath for four to six hours. The relaxing solution is made up of 4 gallons of lukewarm water and 8 pounds of salt. The next step is to wash the skins in 4 gallons of lukewarm water to which 4 to 6 capfuls of Dawn or Joy dish detergent have been added. Then rinse the detergent from the skins.

Make up a pickling solution of 4 gallons of lukewarm water, 2 fluid ounces of Rittel's Saftee-Acid and 4 pounds of salt (2½ cups = 4 lbs.). Place the cleaned and relaxed skins into the pickling solution for a minimum of three days. The pickling solution will safely keep the skins up to two or three weeks or until you are ready to tan them. Examine the skins and flesh them again if needed, then place them back in the pickling bath for another 24 hours.

Make up a neutralizing bath of 4 gallons of lukewarm water and 4 ounces of baking soda (8 tablespoons = 4 oz.). Remove the skins from the pickling solution, allow

The dried skins are first placed in a relaxing bath to soften, then rinsed well.

them to drain for 30 to 40 minutes, then place the skins in the neutralizing bath and let them soak for 30 minutes, stirring frequently. Remove and rinse in clean water.

Now you're ready to tan. Mix up a tanning solution of 4 gallons of lukewarm water, 2 pounds of salt (1¼ cups = 2 lbs.) and 4 ounces of Rittel's EZ-100 (12 tbsp. = 4 oz.). First mix the water and EZ-100, then add the salt. Check the solution for pH using pH strips. If the pH is higher than 4.0, add a very small amount of acid to the solution. If the pH is too low, dissolve some baking soda in a little water and add a small amount. Each time you add anything, stir, let sit for 30 minutes and then recheck the pH. When you reach 4.0, place the skins in the tanning solu-

They are then placed in a pickle solution, removed, shaved to thin as needed, degreased if needed and returned to the pickle bath.

tion and allow them to tan for 16 to 18 hours. Weight them down to make sure they are immersed and stir occasionally. After tanning, remove the skins, rinse them lightly and allow them to drain for 20 to 30 minutes.

After draining, mix 1 part Rittel's ProPlus Oil and 2 parts hot tap water. Do not boil the oil. Apply this mixture to the flesh side of the skin with a paintbrush. After oiling, fold the skins flesh-to-flesh, fur-to-fur and set the skins aside to soak up the oil for three to four hours.

After allowing the skin to "sweat" in the oil, open them up and hang them flesh-side out, outside over a clean clothesline to dry. Usually this will take two to three days. As the skin begins to dry, work it with your hands, pulling and stretching to pull apart and "break" the fibers. As you work the skin, it will dry completely. Use a shoe-shining motion over the back of a chair, a board held in a vise, or a breaking stake. Work the skin until it is soft and dry.

When the skin is completely soft and dry, brush and comb out the fur. For an extra-clean, fluffy fur, work cornmeal into the fur and blow or shake it out. Finish off the leather side by sanding away any small pieces of skin. The result is a beautiful, soft white leather.

Oxalic Acid

Another good and fairly simple immersion tan for small game utilizes oxalic acid. Mix the liquor according to the formula in the chapter on formulas. This formula is caustic and poisonous, so take all precautions in mixing and

After the pickle bath and rinsing, the skins are then placed in the chosen tanning formula for the appropriate time.

using it. Allow the skins to soak in the solution for about 24 hours. Make sure the skins are weighted down so they don't float out of the solution, and stir the solution often. Remove after 24 hours and wash in a solution containing a cup of borax to each gallon of water. Then rinse in several changes of clean water. Partially dry, stretch and oil the flesh side lightly.

Salt and Acid

One of the oldest forms of tanning fur-on hides is salt and acid. This is actually called tawing. The skins will take on moisture in damp weather, so the method should only be used for wall hangings or purposes where they won't get wet. Make up the formula as described in the formula chapter. Be very careful with the acid: Don't breathe the fumes and avoid getting any of the solution on your body or clothing. Dissolve the salt into the water, then very carefully pour in the acid, stirring as you pour. Use only glass or plastic containers.

Once the solution has cooled, place the relaxed and washed skin in the solution and weight it down so it won't float. Allow the skin to tan for one to three days. Make sure you keep the skin or skins stirred regularly so they tan evenly. Check for thorough tanning by cutting off a sliver of the thickest portion, the color should be even.

When the skins have been properly tanned, squeeze out the excess water. Do not wring the skins, as this causes deep creases. Place the skins in a neutralizing wash of 1 ounce borax to each gallon of water. Stir the skin in the solution for 15 minutes or so to wash out the tanning solution. Remove, rinse in clean water, then squeeze to remove excess water. Place the skin on a smooth flat surface, use a slicker to remove additional water, then allow the skin to dry. As the skin dries, work it over a breaking stake to soften. Adding a bit of finishing oil to the flesh side helps provide a more supple skin.

Salt-Alum

This tanning solution can be used as a soak or as a paste applied to the skin. Salt-alum is a good choice for coyote, raccoon and other larger critters. Make up a paste by dissolving 1 pound ammonia alum, potash alum, or aluminum sulphate in 1 gallon of water. Dissolve 4 ounces of washing soda (crystallized sodium carbonate) and 8 ounces of salt in ½ gallon of water. Pour the soda-salt solution very slowly into the alum solution, while stirring vigorously. Immerse the skin in the tanning solution for two to five days, depending on the thickness of the skin. Stir the skin and solution several times a day. To check for proper tanning, cut a small sliver off the thickest part of the skin. The skin should be the same color throughout. If the center shows a different color, continue the tanning process a bit longer. Once you're sure the tanning is complete, remove, partially dry by squeezing and tack the skin to a smooth surface. Apply a thin layer of soft soap. Once this has been absorbed, apply a bit of warmed neat's-foot oil. Allow the skin to partially dry, then remove and soften with the beam or stake. The fur can be cleaned with a quick immersion in white gasoline, sawdust added, and the fur cleaned, combed and fluffed.

To use as a "dry-rub" tanning paste, mix enough flour into the tanning liquor to make a thin paste. Add small amounts of flour into a little water first, stirring to prevent lumps. Spread the skin out on a smooth flat surface and tack it down with roofing nails. Using a brush, knife blade or scraper, apply the paste to the skin. The paste should be about ⅛ inch thick. Allow this to stand until the next day then scrape off the paste and reapply a new coating. Two to three coatings applied at daily intervals will tan most skins. Then allow the last coating to stay on for three to four days.

A paste tanning mixture can also be used, applying it to the flesh side of the skin.

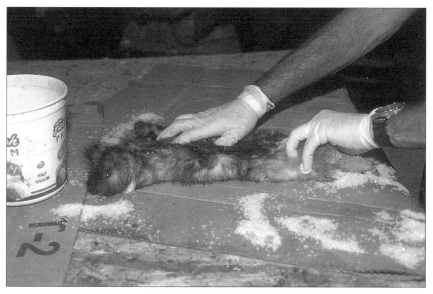

Then the skin is folded flesh-to-flesh and left 24 hours. The paste is removed and replaced each day until the skin is tanned.

Scrape off the paste and wash the skin in a gallon of water to which 1 ounce of borax has been added. Rinse in clean water. Place the skin on the fleshing beam and use a slicker to press out most of the water. Then soften with the stretching process. A bit of neat's-foot oil should be applied at the last of the softening stage.

Combination Chemical and Vegetable Tan

This is another good formula for fur-on skins and is also a paste-type tan using the formula shown in chapter 3. The skin should be well cleaned, degreased and re-laxed. Then slightly dry the fur side so it isn't soaking wet. The flesh side should still be damp. Stretch the skin out and tack it flesh-side-up to a smooth, solid work surface. Apply a ⅛-inch-thick coating, making sure you work all the materials into all of the skin, including the edges. Fold the skin flesh-to-flesh down the middle and allow to sit overnight. The following day scrape off the old paste and reapply new paste. Thin skins will tan in a day or so; thicker skins may require up to three days.

Allow the skin to dry, but before it dries completely, wash out the tanning materials with borax water, then rinse in clean water. Squeeze out the excess water, use a slicker to remove excess water, then apply a bit of oil to the flesh side. Skins such as raccoon with their natural grease do not need the oil step. As the skin dries, work it over a stake to soften.

Rittel's EZ-100 is also excellent for raccoon, fox, coyote and other fur pelts. Another excellent choice is Rittel's Trapline Tanning Kit.

Commercial Tanning Oils

The simplest method of tanning fur-on skins is with one of the tanning oils. Several commercial formulas are available, including TANNIT from the Tandy Company and Deer Hunter's Hide Tanning Formula from Cabela's.

TANNIT provides excellent results on fur skins and is extremely easy to use. Following are general instructions for a skin that has been fleshed, salted and dried:

To begin the tanning process, make a strong solution of 5 pounds of noniodized salt to 5 gallons of water. Make enough of the salt solution to complete immerse the skin. Keep the skin in the salt solution until pliable (about 24 hours on previously salted and dried skins). Remove the

Commercial tanning oil agents are also available. These are rubbed into the flesh side of the skin.

skin and drain. Rinse the skin in clean water to remove excess salt, but do not immerse skin in water any longer than necessary. Some salt needs to remain in the skin for TANNIT to work properly. Rinse to remove the salt crystals on the surface of the skin only.

Greasy skins, such as bear, beaver or raccoon, should be soaked in white gas for about 20 minutes. Be sure to use white gas in an area with lots of ventilation, but no open flames or pilot lights. Outdoors would be best. Rinse in lukewarm water and allow to drain until the skin side is only slightly damp.

Using rubber gloves to protect sensitive skin, apply the TANNIT cream full strength to the flesh (back) side

The skin is folded flesh-to-flesh, left for 24 hours, then opened and allowed to dry slowly.

sparingly, but with an even coating. Heating the TAN-
NIT in a double boiler will greatly assist the penetration. Rub TANNIT in for a few minutes, making sure to
cover the entire skin, including the edges. Lay (flesh-
side up) on a piece of cardboard to prevent molding
and for even drying throughout. Set aside and allow
TANNIT to absorb into the skin. Penetration time varies
with the thickness of the skin and the humidity in the
air. When TANNIT has penetrated completely, some excess cream may "puddle" in a few spots. This can be
scraped off the skin with a butter knife or absorbed
with cornmeal.

The last step involves making the skin pliable. Two
methods can be used—or better yet, a combination of the
methods.

- Method 1: Allow the skin to dry completely at room
  temperature. The back of the skin can then be rasped
  with a coarse-toothed wood rasp or sanded with
  coarse sandpaper until the desired pliability is obtained. Rasping or sanding also fuzzes the back of the
  skin, giving it nice sueded look.
- Method 2: Allow the skin to dry at room temperature.
  Just before the skin has dried out completely, work it
  over the edge of a table, bench beam or tool to
  "break" the fibers. If the skin is still slightly damp, or
  cool to the touch after all areas and edges have been
  worked, allow the skin to dry a little more, then work
  again until completely dry and soft.

I've found the best tactic is to break the skin on the
breaking stake, then go back and sand the thicker areas
with the skin on the fleshing beam, and after it has dried.

Deer Hunter's Hide Tanning Formula from Cabela's is just as easy and effective to use. The best tactic is to start with a fresh, green skin; since the process is so simple, you might find it easy to tan without preserving the skin to tan at a later date. After fleshing, skin out or cut off ears and paws, and split the tail. If the skin has been dried, soak in plain cold water, just long enough to soften.

Salt the flesh side well with noniodized salt. Work plenty of salt into the entire skin including the ears, paws and tail. Fold the salted skin flesh-to-flesh, roll it up and leave it for 24 hours. Scrape off the old salt, rub in new salt and leave for another 24 hours. Scrape and rinse off salt.

Regardless of the tanning methods used, the skin must be softened as it dries gradually by pulling it over a breaking stake in a shoe-shining motion.

Prepare a salt bath by mixing ½ pound of table salt per gallon of hot water. Allow to cool completely, then immerse the skin and leave overnight (12 to 16 hours), or until completely flexible. Remove, rinse in clean water and drain. Using a thin knife or a wire wheel, thin the skin as much as possible, removing any remaining membrane. Wash the skin in warm water with liquid dish soap, such as Dawn or Joy. Very greasy skins, such as bear, beaver or raccoon, should be washed twice with dish soap to remove all grease. Then hang the skin up to drain.

Warm the Hide Tanning Formula in a pan of hot tap water for 30 minutes. The skin should be at room temperature, semidry, but still moist and flexible. Shake the warmed oil well and apply an even layer to the flesh side of the skin.

The flesh side of the skin is finished by sanding or rasping off any rough spots. Adding wooden handles to the rasp makes it easier to use.

Apply with a paintbrush, or by hand wearing latex gloves. Massage the oil firmly into all areas of the skin.

Fold the skin, flesh sides together, and leave overnight (12 to 16 hours). If the skin is a cased skin, just turn the fur out and hang at room temperature, away from direct heat. This will allow the fur to dry while the skin is tanning. After this 12- to 16-hour tanning time, open the flesh side to the air (or if a cased pelt, turn the flesh side out again) and let it dry slowly over a two- to three-day period. As the skin dries, periodically pull and stretch the skin until it is completely dry and soft. If the skin is still stiff in spots, dampen those areas with warm water, reapply the oil and repeat.

The fur should be dried and fluffed by sprinkling with cornmeal or sawdust, then by air drying and beating out the materials, or fluffing in a clothes dryer without a heating element.

When the skin is fully tanned and dry, it can be further thinned with a wire wheel or coarse sandpaper if a higher degree of suppleness is desired. Also, pulling the tanned skin back and forth over a tight hemp rope works very well for softening.

Fluffing and Drying Hair and Fur

Through many of the tanning steps hair and fur have been repeatedly wetted. The fur must be thoroughly dried and fluffed to produce a soft skin showing off a beautiful pelt. Commercial tanneries use large drums with sawdust in the drums to tumble dry the skin, remove unwanted materials and fluff the fur. You can do this at home with an old clothes dryer that has had the heating element removed or a dryer whose heating element doesn't work.

Or you can fluff the fur the hard way. Sprinkle sawdust or cornmeal onto the fur side. Place the skin in a plastic garbage bag and shake it thoroughly to distribute the drying agent. Then remove and further work the agent into the fur. Hang the skin up from a clothesline and use a large barbecue spatula or limber wooden switch to beat out the sawdust. Then comb the skin with a furrier's comb.

FUR-OFF TANNING

Small game skins can also be tanned hair-off. The different animals produce a wide variety of thin skins that are excellent for many purposes. Rabbit skin, for instance, makes very soft and thin gloves. Raccoon and groundhog skins are tougher and, although small, can be used for any number of small leather projects.

All the immersion tans previously mentioned will also work for fur-off tanning of leather. But the first step is to dehair the skin. Use any of the dehairing formulas mentioned in chapter 3 to loosen the hair. Then use a fleshing beam and fleshing knife to scrape the hair or fur off and to "grain" or remove the topmost grain or dead cell layer from the skin.

Oxalic Acid

Another fairly easy tanning for fur-off skins is the oxalic acid formula (see chapter 3). The skins should have been fleshed, grained and dehaired. Mix the solution, taking care because it is caustic and poisonous, and place the skins in the solution. Very small skins will tan in a matter of 24 hours, but most skins will require two to three days to tan thoroughly. Cut off a piece of the skins and check to make sure the tan has penetrated throughout. Once the skins have been tanned, remove and soak them overnight in a neutralizing solution of 1 ounce baking soda to each gallon of water.

Rinse in several changes of clean water and hang to dry. As the skins become partially dry, work them over the fleshing beam or staking knife to stretch and soften. If the skins become dry before they soften, simply moisten the area. A bit of neat's-foot oil rubbed in the flesh side and restaking creates an even more supple skin.

The commercial tans, including Rittel's EZ-100 tan, TANNIT and Cabela's, are also excellent choices for hair-off small game skins. Follow the directions for hair-on tanning once the skin has been dehaired.

CHAPTER

Modern Methods of Tanning Deer and Big Game Hides

Deer skins are one of the most popular tanning materials. Many hunters desire to tan their hard-won trophies into robes, rugs or wall hangings, leaving the hair on the hide. Deer and elk skins also make some of the finest leathers. The skins are relatively light, fairly easy to tan and work, yet provide a very durable and beautiful leather that can be used for any number of projects.

A number of tanning methods and materials may be used on deer, elk and other big game hides including acid tanning, chrome tanning, vegetable tanning and using a variety of other materials. The methods shown in this chapter are modern, although they range from some older, traditional methods to today's latest materials and methods. The following chapter describes the venerable ancient methods of tanning deer skins.

HAIR-OFF TANNING

The first step is to soak the fleshed and preserved skins in a relaxing bath of 1 ounce borax for every gallon of

White-tailed deer—as well as elk—are one of the most popular animals for home tanning of the hides.

water needed to cover the hides. Leave the hides in the relaxing bath for three to five days. Then place the skin or skins in a liming or dehairing solution. Any one of the formulas or materials described in chapter 3 can be used for this process. It will take from a couple of days to a week or more to completely loosen the hair and epidermis so it can easily be removed. The length of time depends on the size of the hide and the weather. Incidentally, in most processes you can do more than one hide at a time. Weight the hide or hides down in the solution and stir several times each day to make sure all parts of the hides are equally treated and there are no folds where the chemicals can't get to the hide. Occasionally, and wearing rubber gloves, pull the hide up out of the solution. Grasp the hair and give it a tug. When it pulls away easily by the handful, you're ready to dehair.

Dehairing

Dehairing is actually one of the messiest chores in tanning. Wear old clothes, rubber boots, a rubber apron, rubber gloves and eye protection. Place the hide, hairside up, on a large, outside fleshing beam. Hold the hide in place with your belly and, with the sharp edge of the fleshing knife, use push strokes away from you to scrape off the loose hair and the epidermis. Most of the hair should come off easily—in fact, it should come off in sheets. If the hair doesn't come off easily, you may need to place the hide back in the solution. Quite often the hair doesn't release very easy around the edges of the hide. Take your time and make sure to get off all hair. Hides from older animals that have wrinkles on the neck and shoulder require extra care in dehairing these areas. Regardless of the effort, be sure to remove all the hair. It's disappointing to tan a hair-off hide only to find a tuft or two of hair remaining after the tanning job. (Any remaining hair will have to be removed by shaving.) As the hair is being removed, you should also see a fatty-looking, cream-colored layer of wet materials come off with the hair. This is the epidermis skin layer and must also be removed completely from the hide for a good tan. Examine the entire hide in good light to make sure there are no spots where the thin epidermis layer is still attached. If the skin begins to dry slightly in hot weather, then it

After fleshing and preserving, the next step in making a leather hide is to soak the skin in a lime or dehairing solution, then scrape the hair off with the skin draped over a fleshing beam.

Use a fleshing knife and push strokes to scrape off all the hair and the epidermis skin layer as well.

Keeping the fleshing knife sharp makes it easier to flesh or dehair hides.

becomes hard to remove the epidermis layer. Moisten the skin with just a bit of water and continue dehairing.

Neutralizing

When the skin is thoroughly dehaired, place it in a neutralizing bath to stop the alkaline action of the lime or dehairing chemicals. A neutralizing solution can consist of 1 quart of vinegar to 3 gallons of water, or 6 ounces of lactic acid powder to 3 gallons of water. Allow the hide or hides to soak in this solution for 24 hours, occasionally stirring to make sure all portions of the hide are neutralized. Then rinse the hides in several changes of clean water.

The hides are now ready for the pickle bath. Or you can freeze the fleshed and dehaired hides at this point to tan at a later time.

Pickling

Regardless of the method of tanning used, the way to begin the next step is to soak the hides in the pickle bath. Pickle baths are used to raise the acidity of the hides and to further soften them for tanning. Any one of the pickle formulas mentioned in chapter 3 can be used. The following information is for using Rittel's Saftee-Acid as a pickle. This material is great for pickling and adjusting the pH. Saftee-Acid is practically odorless, with no caustic fumes, and is nonpoisonous.

First step is to weigh the skins. For every pound of wet, drained skin weight, use 2 quarts of water. For each

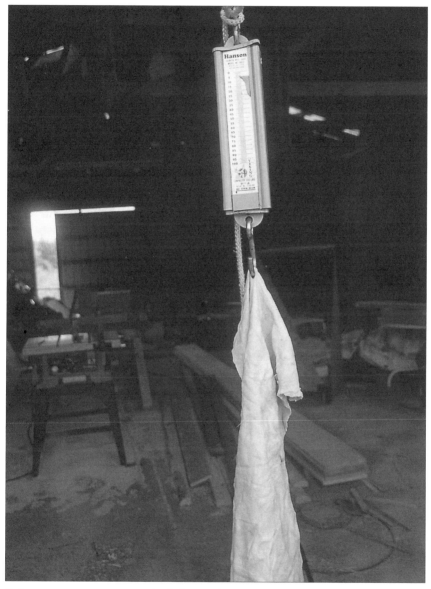

Before most tanning steps, the hide should be soaked in a neutralizing bath, then washed, drained and weighed.

The hide or hides are first placed in a pickling bath, removed and thinned or shaved, then placed back in the pickling bath until ready to tan.

gallon of pickle solution needed, use 1 gallon of water, 1 pound of noniodized salt and ½ fluid ounce of Rittel's Saf-tee-Acid.

This solution should give a pH level of about 1.0 according to the instructions with the acid. As long as the pickle solution is held below 2.0 (normally it varies between 1.1 and 1.5) pH, you should have no problems. The solution will remain very stable—but it's wise to check the pH level daily. Leave the skins in the pickle solution for three days until they are completely pickled.

Remove the skins, drain and rinse out the pickle solution. Shave the flesh side of the skin to thin and even it out. Return the skin to the pickle solution for another 12 to 24 hours. Actually the skins can be left in the pickle solution until you are ready to neutralize and tan the hides. According to Bruce Rittel of Rittel's Tanning Supplies, they have safely left skins in the pickle for up to four weeks with no harm.

Neutralizing

Make up a neutralizing solution of 1 ounce of baking soda to each gallon of water needed to completely immerse the skins. Place the skins in the neutralizing solution and stir them around for 15 to 30 minutes. Rinse out the neutralizing solution and allow the skins to drain.

The hides are removed from the pickling bath, washed and allowed to drain.

Tanning

One of the easiest modern-day tanning methods utilizes Rittel's EZ-100 tanning solution. EZ-100 provides a very durable, white, soft and stretchy leather from deer and elk. And it's a powdered Syntan tanning agent that eliminates environmental and personal handling problems. EZ-100 contains no metallic components but is a synthetically manufactured sulphonic acid agent.

EZ-100 tans best at a pH of 4.0. Check the pH level before placing the skins into the solution and also check 30 minutes later. If the pH is lower than 4.0, add very small amounts of baking soda or sodium acetate. If the pH is higher than 4.0, add small amounts of the pickle,

The hides are then placed in the tanning chosen formula for the amount of time required.

dissolved citric acid or white vinegar. When mixing the tanning solution, first add the EZ-100 and stir until dissolved, then add the salt needed. If mixing a solution for more than one hide, add all the hides to the solution at the same time, not one at a time three or four hours later. EZ-100 is a fast tanner, and the initial skins may deplete the tan before the last skin is placed in the solution. The solution may be mixed in one of two ways—based on the wet drained weight of the hides or on the water volume needed to completely submerge the hides.

• EZ-100 tanning formula based on wet drained weight: After neutralizing the skins and draining them for one hour, weigh the hides to get their wet, drained weight. Use this weight to calculate the amount of tanning solution needed. This is the most accurate and least wasteful method. For every pound of wet, drained weight, mix 2 quarts of water, ½ ounce (4½ level teaspoons) of EZ-100 and 4 ounces of salt.

• EZ-100 tanning formula based on water volume: Neutralize the skins and drain them for one hour. Mix enough solution to completely submerge the skins. For every gallon of water needed to cover the hides, mix in 1 ounce (3 level tablespoons) of EZ-100 and 8 ounces of salt.

It is extremely important not to overcrowd the skins when using the water volume formula. For either solution, keep the solution at a comfortable room temperature or between 65 and 75 degrees F. and leave the skins in the tanning solution for 16 to 20 hours. Almost all skins will thoroughly tan within 24 hours. *Never overtan.* After 24 hours, pull the skins from the tanning solution. Rinse and then allow the skins to drain for 20 minutes, *no longer.*

When the skins have drained for 20 minutes, lay them out flat, flesh-side up. Apply a hot oil-water mixture to the flesh side using a paintbrush. For best results, use 1 part Rittel's ProPlus Oil to 2 parts hot tap water. Apply the oil-water mixture while the mixture is still hot and the skin is at a comfortable room temperature. Apply the mixture carefully along the edges and around any holes. When oiled, fold the skin flesh-to-flesh and lay it aside in a warm area to "sweat" for four to six hours.

Open the skin and hang it up to dry. Drying time will depend on the thickness of the flesh, but usually takes one to two days. When the skin is almost 95 percent dry, begin to work and stretch the fibers with your hands or a staking tool. Work the fibers until the skin is completely dry. If it dries too fast, dampen the flesh side with a sponge, put it in a plastic bag, let it cool or refrigerate it overnight and then hang it to dry the next day. Again work the skin when it is almost 95 percent dry.

When the flesh side is completely dry, use sandpaper or a rasping sheet to clean up the flesh side and give it a professional look. Trim away any ragged edges.

CHROME TANNING

Chrome tanning produces excellent leather, but leather with a bluish cast. The finished skin can be dyed with brown or other colors of leather dyes after the tanning process. All chemicals for this process must be of good

A wide variety of tanning formulas can be used. Shown are the chemicals for a chrome tan.

quality and carefully measured. The tanning solution should be made at least two days before it is to be used. Follow the instructions on mixing the solution in chapter 3. The formula given is for two to three deer hides, weighing not more than 30 pounds total.

After the solution has set for two days, stir it thoroughly, then pour one-third of the stock solution into a clean, 30-gallon plastic barrel or garbage can. The best method is to suspend the hides in the solution with wires hooked over the barrel edges supporting dowels suspended in the solution. Stir the solution at least every hour or so the first day, moving the hides about so they tan uniformly. Leave the hides in the solution for two to

The materials must be kept well stirred and submerged in the tanning solution.

three days, stirring frequently. Remove the hides and add the second one-third of the stock solution, mixing it well with the solution already in the barrel. Place the hides back in the barrel and leave for another day or two. Again, stir the solution and move the hides about for uniformity of tanning. Remove the hides and add the final one-third of the solution to the solution in the barrel. Add the hides and again stir the solution frequently.

Test the skin to make sure it is tanned by cutting off a sliver from the thickest portion of the skin. If the greenish or bluish color goes all the way through, the tanning is complete. You can also boil a piece of skin. If it curls up, or becomes hard and rubbery, the tanning is not finished and the hides must be tanned a few days longer.

Once the tanning is complete, remove the hides from the solution and wash in several changes of water. Place the hides in a solution of 1 pound of borax to 20 gallons of water. Leave for 24 hours, stirring frequently.

Remove and soak the hides in clean water for another 24 hours. Remove the hides and allow to drain, then oil and finish.

Caution: Proper disposal of the tanning solution is important. Check with your local waste management authorities for proper disposal of the solution. It can be poisonous to pets and livestock and harmful to the soil because of the metals involved.

I've had good success using Rittel's Chrome-Tan products. Bruce Rittel suggests pickling the hides before using Rittel's Chrome-Tan products. Bruce says he personally prefers using a formic acid pickle at a 2.5 pH level. The following advice is for using the Rittel's Chrome-Tan and is for skins previously pickled at a pH level of 2.5.

Weigh the skins to be tanned after they have drained for 30 minutes. Record this weight—this is the drained weight of the skins. For every pound of drained weight, mix a solution of 2 quarts of water and 1 ounce of salt. Place the skins in the salt solution and allow them to soak for 30 minutes. While the skins soak, mix the chrome tanning solution. For every 1 pound of drained hide weight, mix a solution of 1 pint of hot tap water (110 to 120 degrees F.) and 2 ounces of Rittel's Chrome-Tan.

Keep this tanning solution separate. After the skins have soaked for 30 minutes in the salt-water solution, remove them, add one-half of the tanning solution concentrate

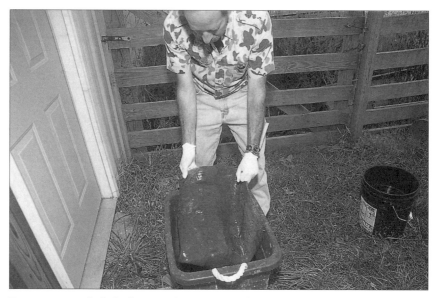

Removing an elk hide from a chrome bath. Chrome tanned hides are bluish in color.

to the salt solution and mix thoroughly. Place the skins back into this solution and allow them to soak for 12 hours. After a 12-hour soak, remove the skins and pour the remaining portion of the tanning solution concentrate into the salt–tanning solution mix. Check the pH level. Ideally it should test between 3.6 and 3.8 for a complete chrome fixation. Use borax to adjust the pH level if necessary. Allow the skins to tan overnight (16 to 18 hours) after returning them to the solution.

After tanning overnight, remove and allow the skins to drain for one to two hours. Wash the skins in a neutralizing bath of borax or sodium bicarbonate. This will raise the pH of the skins to within a more compatible tanning oil range. After neutralizing, the skins are ready for oiling and finishing.

GLUTARALDEHYDE TANNING

The preserved skin should be soaked in a relaxing solution, rinsed, allowed to drain for about an hour, then weighed. For each pound of deer hide use 5 quarts of water (at approximately 85 degrees F.) and 2½ fluid ounces of glutaraldehyde (25 percent commercial solution). Prepare the mixture by pouring the water into a large plastic garbage can or barrel. Add ½ pound of noniodized salt for each gallon of water and stir with a wooden paddle until the salt is thoroughly dissolved. Measure the glutaraldehyde and carefully pour it into the salt solution, stirring as you pour until it dissolves.

Caution: Glutaraldehyde is an irritant. Do not inhale the vapors, or allow it to contact your eyes or skin. Work with adequate ventilation and wear rubber gloves, long pants and a long-sleeved shirt or jacket, a rubber apron and safety glasses.

Carefully lower the skins into the solution to avoid splashing the solution on you. The skins tan best suspended in the solution, but make sure they are totally immersed. Stir the solution for 5 to 10 minutes once the hides are all in place. Then stir a minute or two each hour throughout the day. Keep the container covered while not stirring. The skins should be stirred in the same fashion over the next three days. As the skin tans, it begins to turn yellow. Check for tanning completion at the

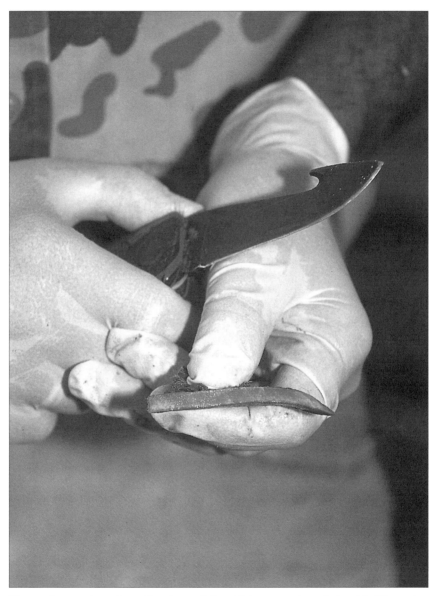

To test for tanning, slice off a piece of the thickest portion of the skin. The color should be uniform throughout the thickness of the hide.

end of three days. After tanning, wash in a neutralizing solution, then oil and finish.

OILING, SOFTENING AND FINISHING TIPS

Regardless of the method used, skins tanned in the above methods must be oiled. Rittel's ProPlus Oil, mixed 1 part oil to 2 parts hot tap water, is an excellent choice. Or you can mix neat's-foot oil half with warm water, adding 1 ounce of household ammonia to 3½ ounces of the neat's-foot oil–water mix. About 7 ounces of either mix will oil a standard-sized deer hide, which weighs about 10 pounds.

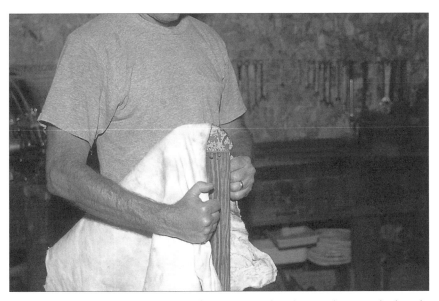

Allow the skin to dry. As it dries, soften it over a breaking stake or stake bench, or with a breaking frame and shoulder stake.

Allow the drained skin to dry to the damp stage, then lay the skin flesh-side up on a smooth flat surface. Apply the warm oil mixture with a brush and rub in by hand wearing rubber gloves. Apply half the solution evenly over the hide and work it well into all edges. Allow the hide to sit for 30 minutes, then add the second half of the solution, also rubbing it in. Lay the skin on a cardboard surface and cover with a plastic garbage bag, or fold the skin over flesh-to-flesh and allow it to sit overnight. The following day hang or drape the skin over an object and allow it to dry. Do not allow the skin to dry thoroughly. As the skin begins to dry, but is still damp, it's time to begin the stake work or "breaking" the skin.

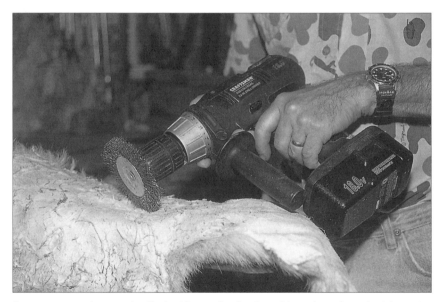

For more suppleness, the flesh side can be further thinned or shaved with a wire brush after the skin has dried.

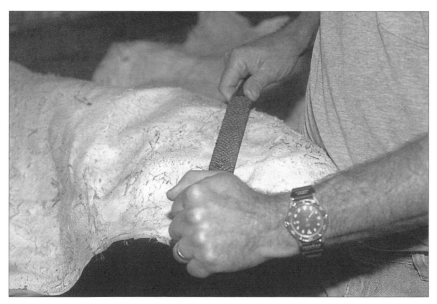

A carpenter's wood rasp can also be used to shave and soften the flesh side of the hide.

Hair-off deer skins are small and lightweight enough to be easily staked on a bench or floor stake. Some elk hides require a staking frame and shoulder stake. Regardless, there's work involved for a good, supple skin. The work can also be quite tiring on your shoulder and arm muscles. I like to work at the staking process for a few minutes, leave it for another chore or a break, then go back. Using this method, it may take a day or longer to thoroughly dry and soften the skin. While the skin is still damp, it will feel cool. As it becomes drier you won't notice the coolness.

Oil-Based Tanning Solutions

The oil-based tanning solutions such as TANNIT from Tandy Leather and Cabela's Deer Hunter's Hide Tanning Formula can also be used to make excellent buckskin-type leather. Both products create a white leather that is soft and very supple. Both are also very simple and easy to use.

Following are the general instructions for tanning a hide with TANNIT. The hide should have been fleshed, salted and dried, limed, dehaired and neutralized.

Make a strong solution of 5 pounds of noniodized salt to 5 gallons of water. Make enough of the salt solution to

Commercial oil-based tanning agents can be used to easily tan deer hides. Hides are first salted, then washed, then the tanning agent applied.

completely immerse the hide. Keep the hide in the salt solution until pliable (at least 24 hours), then remove the hide and drain. Use a sharp fleshing knife to shave and thin the hide and to ensure all membrane is removed and the hide is as thin as possible. Rinse the it in clean water to remove excess salt, but do not immerse it in water any longer than necessary. Salt needs to remain in the hide for TANNIT to work properly. Rinse to remove salt crystals on the surface of the hide only.

Using rubber gloves to protect sensitive skin, apply the TANNIT cream full strength to the flesh (back) side. Apply sparingly, but with an even coating. Heating the TANNIT in a double boiler will greatly assist the penetration. Rub in for a few minutes, making sure to cover the entire hide, including the edges. Lay (back-side up) on a piece of cardboard to prevent molding and for even drying throughout. Set aside and allow TANNIT to absorb into the hide. Penetration time varies with the thickness of the hide and humidity in the air. When TANNIT has penetrated completely, some excess cream may "puddle" in a few spots. This can be scraped off the hide with a butter knife or absorbed with cornmeal.

The last step involves making the skin pliable. Two methods can be used—or better yet a combination of the methods.

• Method 1: Allow the hide to dry completely at room temperature. The back of the hide can then be rasped with a coarse-toothed wood rasp or sanded with coarse sandpaper until the desired pliability is obtained. Rasping or sanding also fuzzes the back of the hide, giving it sueded look.

- Method 2: Allow the hide to dry at room temperature. Just before the hide has dried completely, work it over the edge of a table or breaking stake to "break" the fibers. If the hide is still slightly damp, or cool to the touch after all areas and edges have been worked, allow it to dry out a little more, then work again until completely dry and soft.

Deer Hunter's Hide Tanning Formula from Cabela's is just as easy to use. Again, the hide should have been salted, fleshed, limed, dehaired and neutralized.

Prepare a salt bath by mixing ½ pound noniodized table salt per gallon of hot water needed to completely

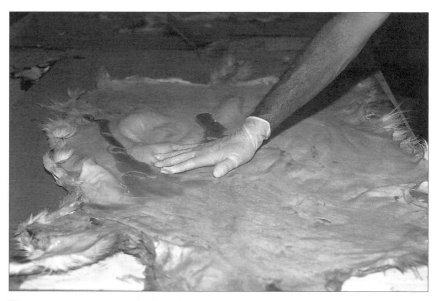

The tanning agent is rubbed well into the flesh side, then the hide folded flesh-to-flesh and left overnight. As the hide dries, it is staked in the normal fashion.

cover the hides. Allow to cool completely, then immerse the hide and leave overnight (12 to 16 hours), or until completely flexible. Remove, rinse in clean water and drain. Using a thin knife or a wire wheel, thin the skin as much as possible, removing any remaining membrane. Wash the skin in warm water with liquid dish soap, such as Dawn or Joy, added. Very greasy skins, such as bear, beaver or raccoon, should be washed twice with dish soap to remove all grease. Then hang the skin up to drain.

Warm the Hide Tanning Formula in a pan of hot tap water for 30 minutes. The skin should be at room temperature, semidry, but still moist and flexible. Shake the warmed oil well and apply an even layer to the flesh side. Apply with a paintbrush, or by hand wearing latex gloves. Massage the oil firmly into all areas of the skin.

Fold the skin, flesh sides together, and leave overnight (12 to 16 hours). After 12 to 16 hours of tanning time, open the flesh side to the air. As the hide dries, periodically pull and stretch the skin until it is completely dry and soft. If the skin is still stiff in spots, dampen those areas with warm water, reapply the oil and repeat.

When the skin is fully tanned and dry, it can be further thinned with a wire wheel or coarse sandpaper if a higher degree of suppleness is desired.

No additional oil is required using the above two products. Both turn out a very white leather. If you desire more of a buckskin color you can dye the hide using a mild solution of quebracho. Or the hide can be smoked as described in the following chapter on ancient tanning methods.

Deer and other big game hides can be tanned with the hair on for robes or rugs.

HAIR-ON TANNING

Deer and other big game hides can also be tanned leaving the hair on the hide. All the tanning materials and procedures previously mentioned will work equally well for hair-on tanning. Follow the same basic steps, except the liming and dehairing step is left out. Oiling and finishing are done only to the back or flesh side of the hide, and the hair may need to be cleaned and degreased on some animals.

CHAPTER

9

Making Buckskin

W
hen most of us think of buckskin, we think of deer hides tanned in the Native American fashion, including smoking. Actually many other hides were tanned by the Native Americans in the same manner, including antelope, elk and buffalo. These skins were used for clothing, footwear, headgear, bags, tipi covers and other items. Buckskin can be made fairly easily by the home tanner, and is a durable and beautiful leather. It's a must if you're into "buckskinning."

Although the old methods varied somewhat with different regions of the country, the basic tanning was the same. A lot of time and hard work is required to create good buckskin. On the other hand, few materials or tools are required. About halfway through writing this book, I found several Native American flint hide scrapers near my home in the Ozarks. I took that as an omen, and experimented with them on hides. The tools were amazingly effective at scraping and fleshing. In fact, they did as well, if not better, than the tools I made using "modern" materials. Bone scrapers were also used by Native Americans. Not everyone has access to artifacts, nor are they needed to work buckskin. The modern tools needed

Ancient tanning methods, though time-consuming, can also be used to tan leathers, including making buckskin.

are described in the tool chapter. You'll need a stretching frame, or a log for a fleshing beam, a scraper and a softening tool.

Traditional buckskin making is not really tanning in the sense of modern-day tanning. Rather, the technique consists of softening and separating the fibers in the animal skin by mechanical means. The mechanical means translates into a lot of backbreaking work. The application of grease followed by smoke was used to preserve the skin. Buckskin does not have the suppleness of tanned leather when it gets wet. It can, however, be made supple again by working the dried buckskin with your hands.

Dehairing and Fleshing

The first step is to dehair the hide. Traditional buckskin, however, was not chemically dehaired. One method was to lace the hide to a wooden frame and use a scraper to first remove all fat, meat and the membrane from the flesh side. Another Native American method was to peg the skin to the ground for this task. Then the hair was removed by dry scraping. It takes a lot of effort to dry scrape the hair from a hide. You really have to put your back into it. If dry scraping, any holes in the skin must be temporarily sewn together or you will make them larger with the pressure exerted on the skin. Another method is to simply drape the skin over a log of a convenient size and dry scrape. Some purists believe dry scraping produces the finest buckskin; however, it is also the hardest method.

First step is to dehair the hide. One method is dry scraping, but an easier method is loosening the hair with wood ashes, then wet scraping.

In other instances the skins were first soaked in warm water to plump them before the scraping process. Deer hair slips fairly easily, and these hides were often simply left in the warm water until the hair began to slip.

The easiest method of dehairing is to first soak the skins in a weak solution of lye water. The lye water is produced from wood ashes. This allows the hair to slip and plumps the skin for easier working. About 3 gallons of fresh, dry, white wood ashes, without any charcoal chunks, are required to do a deer hide. Add about 1½ gallon of ashes to each 5 gallons of water needed to cover the hides in a plastic or wooden tub. Stir thoroughly to dissolve the ashes. Place an egg in the ashes; it should

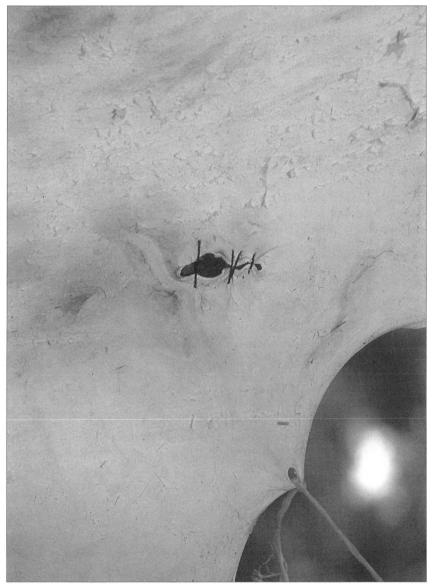

If the skin is to be dry-scraped on a frame stretcher, any holes should first be sewn shut.

float. If the egg doesn't float, add more ashes. You can also use ¼ cup of lye dissolved in 10 gallons of water. Mix the solution as described in chapter 3. Use extra caution when using the lye.

Place the hide in the solution and weight it down with a rock so it doesn't float. Keep the hide in the solution until the hair slips easily when pulled. Wear rubber gloves for this task. Stir the solution several times each day to keep the hide evenly "working." Although the lye dehairs hides the quickest, you can see why dry scraping was commonly used. Working with the lye water before rubber gloves would not have been fun.

As with modern-day tanning, it's extremely important to get all of the epidermis or upper grain layer removed

For frame scraping, holes are punched around the perimeter of the skin. An awl can be used over a block of wood.

The skin is then laced to a frame. The skin is fleshed and scraped to remove all hair, flesh and membranes.

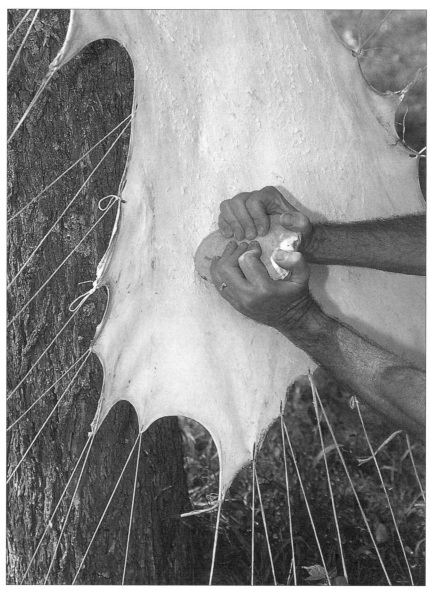

Shown is the use of an ancient, Native American scraper I found near my home to flesh and remove the membranes.

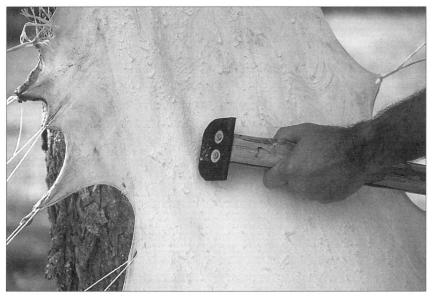

A homemade scraper with a sharpened metal edge can also be used.

for a good buckskin. All flesh, fat and membrane on the flesh side of the hide must be removed as well.

If the hide is dehaired by dry scraping, or only warm water is used, no neutralizing bath is needed. If lye or ashes is used to loosen the hair, a neutralizing bath is needed. The neutralizing bath consists of 10 gallons of water to which 3 gallons of vinegar have been added. Allow the hide to soak overnight, then remove the hide, dump the neutralizing solution and wash the hide in several changes of water. Wash the hide well and wring dry. It is important to remove all water possible from the hide.

Braining

The next step was "braining." Actually a mixture of materials was often used, including brains and liver from the animal killed. Caution: These days with the possibility of chronic wasting disease (CWD), most experts and biologists suggest avoiding contact with brains or spinal fluids of deer or elk. I've substituted calf brains for the deer brains, and calf liver will also work, although not as well as the brain matter.

The brains should be placed in a cloth bag and boiled for about an hour. Do this outside over a camp stove or fish fryer and use an old pot. Remove the bag, retaining the hot liquid. Allow the brains to cool enough to handle the bag, then open the bag and force the brain matter out into a glass or plastic container. Pour half of the brain mat-

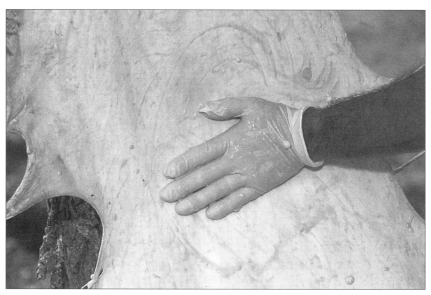

The tanning agents, sometimes brains, are applied to the skin.

The skin is then soaked in a brain solution and all excess liquid squeezed out.

ter back into the cooked liquid. Half of the brain matter is worked into the hide by hand. The other half, mixed in the cooked liquid, is later used to cover the hide.

I've also had good luck simply placing the brains in extremely hot tap water and smashing them with my hands. You will still need enough liquid to cover the hide for the final step; this will require about 2 gallons. Regardless, the brain material must be applied while warm. Rub it thoroughly into the hide on both sides. Then place the hide in a tub and cover with the remaining brain solution. Allow this to sit for several hours or, better yet, overnight. The hide will absorb most of the brain materials.

Remove the hide from the brain solution and thoroughly wring it to remove as much of the moisture as possible. Restring the hide on the stretching frame, then use a softening

The brain matter is forced into the skin and the skin softened with a wooden stake.

tool to thoroughly work the brain material further into the hide and to stretch and break the fibers. Continue to do this every 15 to 20 minutes or so, take a rest and repeat until the hide is soft and dry. This step is best done with the frame in the shade so the hide doesn't dry too quickly.

Another tactic is to wring as much moisture as possible from the hide, then pull it back and forth over a hemp rope strung fairly tautly between trees. A wire cable can also be used for this chore. Or you can work the hide back and forth over a breaking stake such as used for modern-day tanning tactics.

Fat Treating

The fat rendered from bear, beaver, raccoon or pigs can be substituted for the brain matter in making buckskin. To render, the fat should be cut into small pieces and heated over a low flame to cook out the oil or grease. The fibrous material left is strained out and the oil or grease warmed and worked into the hide from both sides. The hides are then worked in the same manner to soften and finish. Brain- and especially fat-treated hides do take on their own "flavor."

Soap Treating

You can also make buckskin from materials that don't have quite the odor. Homemade lye soap is made of animal fats and is the main ingredient. A couple of bars of soap are shaved into approximately ½ gallon of boiling water and allowed to dissolve. Then add this to 3½ gallons of warm water and pour into a tub or barrel. The solution should be very "soapy" feeling. Allow the hide to sit in the solution for three days. Stir the hide frequently to make sure all portions are well soaked. Then remove and rinse the hide in several changes of clean water. Squeeze the hide to remove as much moisture as possible and hang to dry, or place in a stretching frame to dry. As the hide begins to dry, stake it, or rub it with the softening tool if on the frame, to soften the hide until it is almost dry.

Rub a warmed neat's-foot oil solution into the hide, return it to the solution, and leave it for another three days. Remove the hide from the solution and rinse well in several changes of water. Place the hide back on the stretching frame and rework it again until the skin is soft and smooth. Or you can work the hide on a breaking stake or over the hemp rope until soft and smooth.

The skin can be staked, put back on the frame and staked, or worked over a hemp rope or cable to stretch and break the fibers to further soften it.

You can also substitute two bars of naphtha soap shaved into 4 gallons of hot water with a pint of neat's-foot oil added to the mixture. With the oil added to the mixture, you don't need to oil the hide after the first soaking.

Regardless of which material is used, the thoroughly dried hides should be rolled up and stored for a couple of weeks to allow them to cure.

Smoke Curing

The cured hides will have a bright, white appearance and, if allowed to get wet, will dry hard again. The Native Americans took another step—smoke was also used to cure the hides. This not only made the skins more water resistant, but added color and "aroma." I have also smoke-cured deer skins tanned in modern methods to change them from the white stage to a buckskin color and also to add more moisture resistance.

A tripod of thin wooden saplings can be used to smoke the hides. The idea is to create a small and slow fire, feeding it with green, rotten and/or damp wood to maintain a slow smoke. Do not use soft woods that contain pitch or resin for the fire; the fire should also not be hot enough to cook the skins. One method of making sure the fire doesn't get too hot is to dig a trench under and out from the tripod, build a fire in the trench and cover the trench with boards. Leave the area under the tripod open and the smoke will come up through the opening. The skins are fastened on the tripod with nails or string. First one side of the skin is smoked, then the hides are turned over and the other side is smoked.

Final step in creating buckskin is to smoke it to make the skin waterproof and to create the traditional buckskin color.

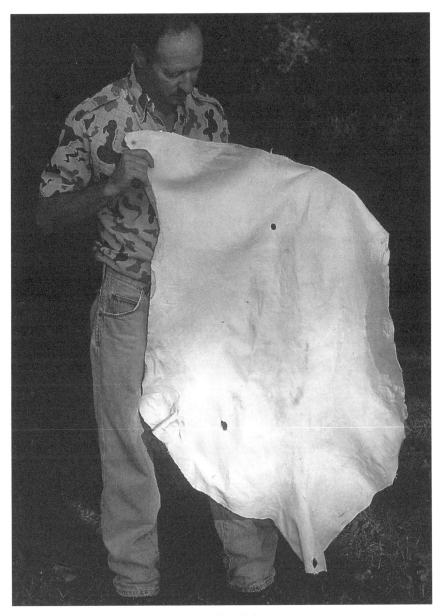

The resulting brain-tanned and smoked buckskin.

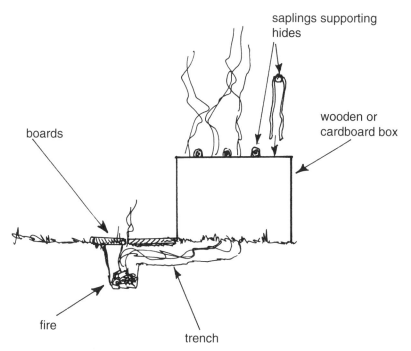

A smoking fire trench makes it easier to keep a cool smoke to the hides.

A wooden box can be built—or even a large card-board box can be used for smoking, as in smoking meat. Place the box over the opening at the end of the trench, lay the hides across sticks in the top of the box and smoke the hides. The amount of smoking time will vary from a day to three or more days. When smoked prop-erly, the hides will turn a nice tan color.

Once the smoking is complete, rinse the hides and then stake again to further soften. The flesh side of the hides should be finished by rubbing with thin sandpaper. The Native Americans thinned the thicker portions of the hides by working them with sharp shells and flint or bone scrapers.

10

Tanning Domestic Hides and Skins and Hair-On Robes

T he majority of today's commercial leathers are tanned from domestic animals, including cows, calves, bulls, sheep, goats and even pigs. The smaller animal skins are treated in much the same manner as deer and small game hides.

WOOL-ON SHEEP SKIN

A tanned wool skin makes a great robe or garment lining and can easily be tanned with Rittel's Ewe-Tan-It Sheepskin Tanning Kit. The kit contains EZ-100, a synthetically manufactured sulphonic acid agent with no metallic components.

The animal should be skinned, the skin laid out flat and allowed to cool for an hour or so, then fleshed. Make sure to wipe away any bloodstains, as they will be almost impossible to remove after tanning. These light skins can be stretched and air dried, and then relaxed later for tanning. Bruce Rittel of Rittel's Tanning Supplies recommends for best results to first salt the hide to preserve it.

The most common source of leather is domestic animals such as cattle.

When ready to tan the wool skin, place the skin in a strong brine solution of 2 pounds of noniodized salt to every gallon of cool water needed to completely submerge the skin. Or use 4 tablespoons Rittel's Ultra Soft Relaxing agent to each gallon of water needed to cover the skins. Soak the skins for 24 hours or longer.

Remove, rinse in several changes of water and place directly into the pickle bath. Rittel suggests a pickle made of Rittel's Saftee-Acid. For every gallon of solution needed to completely submerge the skin, mix 1 gallon of lukewarm water, ½ fluid ounce of Saftee-Acid (4½ teaspoons) and 1 pound of noniodized salt (½ cup = 1 lb.).

After mixing the solution, test the pH level. The pH should read below 2.0. Measure the salt content using a salinometer. It should read 40 percent or higher. Place the

Rittel's EWE-TAN-IT SHEEPSKIN TANNING KIT makes tanning sheepskin easy.

wool skins into the solution and allow them to pickle for a minimum of three days. When thoroughly pickled the wool skins will appear translucent and milky-white colored.

Remove the skins from the pickle solution and allow them to drain for an hour. While the skins drain, prepare a neutralizing bath. For every gallon of water needed to submerge the wool skins, add 1 ounce of sodium bicarbonate, or 1 ounce of sodium acetate. Place the wool skins in this solution and soak them for about 20 minutes, stirring often. After neutralizing, rinse thoroughly in several changes of water and allow the skins to drain for an hour.

Because tanning agents are extremely sensitive to pH, always check the pH of the solution before adding the skins. Then adjust as needed, adding a small amount of baking soda if pH is low or a small amount of Saftee-Acid or pickle if pH is high.

Rittel's EZ-100 tanning formula can be mixed either by the weight of the drained hide or the water volume needed to submerge the hides.

The drained weight formula requires the hides to be weighed after draining them for one hour. For each pound of drained hide weight mix 1 gallon of water, 8 ounces of noniodized salt and ½ ounce EZ-100 (4½ level teaspoons).

Or after draining the neutralized wool skins for one hour you can simply submerge the skins in enough solution to completely cover the hides. The formula is based on the amount of water used to cover the hides. For every gallon of water used, add 8 ounces of noniodized salt and 1 ounce of EZ-100 (3 level tablespoons).

When using the water volume formula, it's extremely important not to crowd the wool skins. For either formula, keep the solution at a comfortable room temperature of between 65 and 75 degrees F. Leave the wool skins in the tanning solution for 12 to 16 hours. Do not leave the hides longer than 24 hours—do not overtan. Remove the skins from the tanning solution, allow them to drain for two to four hours, but do not allow them to dry.

Do not tumble wool skins in dry sawdust like other furs and hair-on skins. The sawdust is almost impossible to remove from the skins. If you have an old washer available, use the spin cycle to remove moisture. It's necessary to remove surface moisture from both the wool and the flesh side, but do not dry the skin completely before oiling.

Lay the drained and fluffed wool skins flesh-side up on a smooth, flat surface. Apply a hot oil-water mixture to the flesh side using a paintbrush. Use 1 part Rittel's

All the same basic steps are used with domestic hides as for creating other leather. Shown is salting a cowhide.

ProPlus Oil to 2 parts hot tap water. Apply the oil-water mixture while it is still hot to the room-temperature skin. When well oiled, fold the wool skin flesh-to-flesh and lay aside to "sweat" in the oil for four to eight hours.

After the wool skin has sweated in the oil, open it up. "I prefer to tack the wool skin out on a board to dry," says Bruce Rittel. "I use 2- to 3-inch nails and, after I get it tacked in place, I pull the hide up to the ends of the nails, close to the nail heads. This allows for air circulation through the wool."

Drying will depend on the thickness of the skin and the humidity, but usually takes two to six days. When the skin is almost dry, begin to work and stretch the fibers with your hands or a staking tool. Work the fibers until the hide is completely dry. If the wool skin dries too fast, dampen the flesh side with a sponge, put it in a plastic bag, tie it off, keep it cool, and begin to work on it again the next day.

For the most part sheepskins don't need shaving or thinning. Once the flesh side is completely dry, use sandpaper or a rasping sheet to clean up the flesh side. If you find it difficult to comb out the wool—and this can be a problem—you should consider using wool shears to make it a shearling pelt.

Sheepskins can also be tanned using the glutaraldehyde method described in chapter 8. Before tanning the skins must be thoroughly washed in numerous changes of lukewarm soapy water using Joy or Dawn dishwashing soap to remove the grease and materials from the wool. Allow the hide to drain, then rinse in several changes of clean water.

Once the skin has been properly tanned and staked by the above methods, it can be washed in a mild detergent. This can be by hand or machine washed on cold for about five minutes. Spin dry in the washing machine, then hang on a clothesline to further dry. Comb out the wool with a wire dog brush.

HEAVY HIDES

Large cow and bull hides can also be home tanned into leathers, but it takes more work simply because of their large sizes and thickness of the hides. These hides also weigh a great deal more, which makes handling them—for instance, lifting them out of the tanning formulas—much harder. Staking is usually done suspending the hides from a ceiling frame and using a shoulder stake. Because of the size and weight, it's a good idea to cut the hides into two separate pieces down the middle of the back and tan each side separately. A great deal of thinning and shaving is also necessary to home tan these heavy hides into usable garment and other leathers. Use a sharp draw knife and a fleshing beam for the shaving processes.

Chrome Tanning

Chrome tanning is the most common modern method used for these big, heavy hides. The same basic materials and steps as described in chapter 8 are used.

Bark tanning was a favorite method, but chrome tanning is probably the most consistent these days. Shown is a hide draining ready for tanning.

Bark Tanning

Bark or vegetable tanning was a traditional method with heavy leathers, and produces a very durable, water-resistant leather. If going by the old method you must have the time, inclination, patience and desire, but it still produces one of the best tans for this type of leather, which is typically used to make saddles and shoes and boots.

Bark tanning utilizes the tannins in any number of wood species. This includes sumac, gambier, quebracho, mimosa, chestnut or—for the home tanner with a plentiful supply—oak.

Because oak is the most common material for this type of traditional tanning, we'll discuss it first. The tanning solution must be prepared well in advance of use, primarily because of the time and effort required. You'll need about 40 pounds of oak bark. I've found one of the best sources is logging areas where trees have been dropped, skidded and then cut into lengths needed for hauling out. Old firewood with slipping bark also works well. In any case, peel the bark from the logs. The next step is to pulverize the bark as finely as possible. This can be done in a number of ways. If you have access to a farmer's hammer mill, use it to pulverize the bark. Or run the bark through a brush chipper. The latter won't produce quite as fine a material, and the finer the material the better the tanning agent. You can also run the material through a hand-cranked steel gristmill used for grinding flour, but it's a job!

Once the bark has been ground, place it in a 50-gallon wooden or plastic barrel or tub. Add 20 gallons of extremely hot water. Allow the bark to steep for two to three weeks, stirring regularly.

You can home tan heavy hides from cattle—it just takes more work. It's a good idea to split the hides down the back into 2 pieces.

For tanning, pour the solution out through a strainer to remove the larger chunks, then pour back into the barrel. Mix in 2 quarts of vinegar and add the hides. Complete filling the barrel with soft water until the hides are well covered. Allow this solution to stand for a couple of weeks. It's best to suspend the hides and stir the solution regularly each day for even tanning.

While the first solution is steeping, grind and produce another solution of the same amount. Take out 5 gallons of the old tanning agent and add 5 gallons of the new mix. Again, mix in 2 quarts of vinegar and leave for five days.

Repeat this step four times. Then repeat a fifth time, but leave out the vinegar. Finally place the hide in a new tanning solution and leave it for four to six months, depending on the thickness of the leather, and be sure the hide is completely submerged. At the end of six months, remove and cut a sliver off for a tanning test.

If tanned completely through, remove, wash thoroughly, oil, and then stake or break and finish. If not tanned completely through, repeat the tanning process.

Vegetable Extract Tanning

Using a vegetable extract greatly shortens and simplifies the tanning job. The following information is from Rittel's Tanning Supplies for their vegetable extract tanning agent.

Vegetable tanning produces the best results when the skins are placed into the tannage, and the pH level of the skins is above the pH level of the tannage. Dehaired and delimed skins can be placed directly into the tanning solution without pickling, but pickled skins should be neutralize overnight in a borax or sodium bicarbonate solution, to raise the pH level to above 4.5.

Weigh the skins after draining for 30 minutes. For every pound of drained skin weight, mix 2 quarts of water and 1 ounce of noniodized salt. Place the skins in the salt solution and allow them to soak for 30 to 90 minutes.

While the skins soak in the salt solution, mix the vegetable tanning stock solution. For every pound of drained skin weight, mix 1 pint of hot tap water (110 to 120 degrees F.) and 10 ounces of Rittel's powdered vegetable extract.

Allow the vegetable tanning stock solution to cool, then remove the skins from the salt solution and pour a quarter of the vegetable stock solution into the salt solution. Return the skins and allow them to soak overnight. Repeat this for four days until the stock solution is completely poured into the original salt solution. Check the pH level of the solution each time before returning the skins. The pH should read 3.5. If not, raise the pH level using borax or sodium bicarbonate. Allow the skins to soak a total of seven days before checking them for complete tannage. Check for tanning by cutting a small piece from the edge and examining it. It should be evenly colored throughout. If not, return the skins to the solution until they are evenly tanned. When evenly tanned, remove the skins and hang them to drain for one or two hours.

After draining, wash the skins in a neutralizing bath of borax or sodium bicarbonate. This raises the pH level of the skins to a more compatible tanning oil range. Then rinse in several changes of clear water. After neutralizing, the skins are ready for oiling and finishing.

HAIR-ON HEAVY ROBE AND RUG TANNING

Cattle, horses, buffalo (American bison), moose and other large animals, including bear, can also be tanned with the hair on to produce heavy robes or rugs. Even domestic cattle can produce beautiful rugs, especially if they are well marked. Bear and buffalo skins were a tradition with the Native Americans and are also very warm if worn as robes.

Again the process requires quite an effort in staking or breaking the skin. And a hair-on hide is extremely heavy. A hair-on hide from a large animal, and in the wet stage during the soaking processes, can weigh more than 100 pounds.

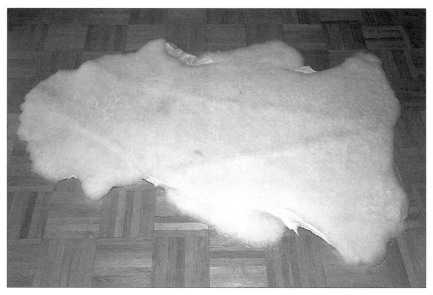

Many domestic animals, including sheep and cattle, can be tanned with the hair on for rugs or robes.

Any number of tanning methods can be used for these heavy hides. In the old days, the hides were pickled, then an oxalic acid tan used. Paste salt-alum tans were also used. Chrome tanning again is the most common commercial method.

The key to soft, supple skins from these heavy hides is proper shaving. "For very soft, supple buffalo skins, they should be shaved two to three times," says Bruce Rittel of Rittel's Tanning Supplies. "Most tanners pull them from the pickle, drain them for 30 to 60 minutes, then shave them and return them to the pickle for another 24 hours. As a rule, the skin will again plump up, and they are shaven again, and again returned to the pickle to plump and are shaven for a third time. This produces a thin, workable skin that's easily staked soft. After the third shaving, the skin is then degreased, washed and rinsed and returned to the pickle for another 24 hours (or up to two weeks) before rinsing and neutralization."

The following information is for tanning a hair-on bison skin, but will work for any long-haired skin to be tanned into a robe. Rittel suggests using their Saftee-Acid pickle. For every gallon of water used, add 1 pound of noniodized salt (½ cup), ½ ounce of Saftee-Acid (4½ teaspoons) plus 8 grams of Rittel's Acid Bate for softer hair. The pH level should be 1.1 to 1.5. Soak the skin in this solution for a minimum of three days or longer. Remove, drain 30 minutes and shave. If necessary, degrease using Rittel's Super Solvent, soaking for one hour. Do a quick wash with a detergent, rinse thoroughly and then place back in the pickling solution for a minimum of 24 hours.

To neutralize, use a baking soda bath to raise the pH of the skin before tanning. Add 1 ounce of baking soda to every gallon of water used and soak the skins for 30 minutes. Then remove, drain one hour, and thoroughly rinse.

Rittel's E-Z 100 Tanning Agent produces a washable skin suitable for robes. Unlike alum or Lutan F, the tannage is very durable and not easily washed out. Mix the following formula for every pound of wet, drained skin weight: 2 quarts of water, 6 ounces of noniodized salt and ½ ounce (4½ teaspoons) of Rittel's EZ-100 tanning agent.

Adjust the pH level of this solution to 4.0 before placing the skin into it. Use a small amount of acid to lower the pH and small amounts of baking soda dissolved in water to raise it. After placing the skins in the tanning solution for one hour, stir, and again check the pH level for 4.0. Stir this solution three or four more times and allow the skins to tan for 16 to 20 hours. Do not overtan. Allowing the skin to soak longer than 24 hours will sacrifice stretchiness. When tanned, remove the skin, allow to drain for 30 minutes, then rinse.

After rinsing, drain again for 30 minutes. Some tanners prefer to lace the skin into a frame after draining and then apply the oil. After oiling, however, the frame should be left horizontal for three to six hours, or until all oil has penetrated, then placed in a vertical position to dry. If not using a frame, open the skin flesh-side up and apply the oil and water mixture thoroughly to all the flesh. For the best results apply Rittel's ProPlus Oil mixed 1 part oil to 2 parts hot tap water and apply using a brush while the mixture is still hot.

Fold the skin flesh-to-flesh and place in a warm area to soak up the oil. Allow the oil to sweat in for three to six hours.

Hang the skin up to dry. It can be toggled onto a stretching frame or laced into a drying frame. Unlike most skins with shorter hair, buffalo skins are usually not tumbled in sawdust because the sawdust is difficult to remove. After the skin is 90 percent dry, begin to stake and soften it. After softening, sand the flesh side to a nice suede and comb out the hair.

These skin robes can be washed, and, according to Rittel, you can machine wash using Woolite and lukewarm water.

11

Rawhide, Latigo and Sole Leather

In addition to leathers, pelts, rugs and robes, hides are also used for a variety of other purposes such as made into rawhide, latigo and sole leather for shoes, belts and harness.

RAWHIDE

Rawhide was a very important product for the Native Americans as well as the settlers. Just about anything that needed to be held together could be held together with rawhide. Rawhide is basically untanned leather and, when dried, is almost rock hard. To be used, rawhide is soaked to be softened, then cut and shaped as desired. It can then be molded over objects and stitched together. When the hide dries it retains the form. The hide also shrinks when dry, thus it made extremely tight bindings.

Most people think of deer or cow hides when rawhide is mentioned. Rawhide, however, can be made of almost any skin. Elk, buffalo, even small game such as woodchuck or beaver can be made into rawhide. If possible, don't use salted hides to produce rawhide.

The steps to producing rawhide are simple and easy. The hide must first be thoroughly fleshed. If the hide has been dried, it should be placed in a relaxing water bath until it softens. Then the hide is drained and placed in a lime bath until the hair slips. When the hair slips, dehair as described in previous chapters.

Spread the hide out on a smooth, flat surface in a cool, dry area. Tack the hide in place, stretching it as much as possible during the stretching process. Once the hide dries, it can be kept forever, stored in a cool, dry place until needed. Pets and wild critters will chew on the rawhide, so it should be kept in a protected place.

You can easily create rawhide at home from either small skins or large hides. Shown is half a cowhide made into rawhide.

When you get ready to use the material, simply soak it in water. It will eventually again become soft.

LATIGO

Latigo leather is rawhide that is cut into strips and well oiled, or greased, then staked or worked to soften the leather. These strips can be used as boot lacings, for braiding into bridles, ropes called riatas, whips and for other lacings, such as snowshoes and even into lacings for garments.

SOLE LEATHER

Heavy leather is used as sole leather for shoes, belting, and for harness. Sole leather can be tanned using traditional chrome or bark tanning methods.

Another traditional method is to make sole leather of rawhide, treating it much the same as latigo. The rawhide material is softened in a water relaxing bath, then allowed to dry to a damp stage. Warmed oil or grease is worked into both sides of the hide. Because of the thickness, sole or harness leather is not staked. Excess oil or grease is removed by slicking the hide with a slicker. Work from the inside out to the edges with the slicker. A great deal of pressure is needed in this step to force the oil into the hide and make it more flexible.

CHAPTER

12

Birds

Tanned or preserved bird skins can be used as a number of items. Preserved skins make great wall decorations, hatbands and decoration for a number of clothing and accessories. The pelts of many birds are also desired by fly tyers. The skins from larger birds, such as ostrich and emu, are tanned into leather for any number of items including belts and boot trim.

SKINNING BIRDS

Proper skinning is extremely important. Bird skins, especially those of smaller, lighter-skinned birds, are very fragile. They tear and cut easily, and the skin can quickly be ruined. Use a very sharp and small knife and work slowly and carefully. For a skin to be used primarily for display you may wish to skin from the back instead of the normal, up-the-belly method. Skinning from the back keeps the breast portion of the bird skin intact. Make the initial starting skinning cut by pinching up the skin and making a small slit. Make the slit just large enough to get the knife blade under the skin. Then make the remaining

Bird skins can be preserved to maintain their beautiful plumage for use as wall hangings or in tying flies, or large bird skins can be tanned as leather.

skin-opening cuts from the underside of the skin. This prevents cutting through delicate feathers.

Carefully pull the skin away from the carcass and use the knife blade to judiciously loosen the meat from the skin as needed. This is particularly necessary around the back and on waterfowl on either side of the top of the breastbone. Skin out the wings, at least to the outer joint. The wing tips will rarely putrefy, except on larger birds. Take your time skinning out the wings, as this requires quite a bit of detail work. Skin to the legs, and around the head if the head has beautiful plummage.

First step is skinning the bird. Using a scalpel, cut around the beak, then make a cut from the top of the head across the back to the tail.

Preserving Bird Skins

The bird skin can be stretched out and well covered with borax for a simple preservation. Make sure the powder is rubbed into all surfaces. The skin should be tacked in place to a board to allow it to dry.

Tanning Bird Skins

Tanning provides a better method of preserving bird skins. A simple salt-alum paste mixture can be used for skins used only for display. Mix the tan as per the formula in chapter 3 and apply to the stretched and tacked skin. Allow to sit for three days, then scrape off and apply a new coating of the tanning paste. Allow this to sit for three more days then scrape off the excess material. Skins tanned in the method will eventually harden and turn brittle with age.

For a longer-lasting tan, use Rittel's Bird-Tan. This actually tans and lends strength to the skin. The bird skin will whiten out when dry. Rittel's recommends the following steps.

Wash the bird skin in a bath of Rittel's Relaxer/Washer/Degreaser and cool water. Use 2 capfuls of the material to every gallon of water. This is also an excellent blood remover. Be sure to scrub away any bloodstains at this time, then rinse in clean water.

Some birds, particularly waterfowl, have extremely greasy skins. Degrease the skin in a bath of 9 tablespoons of Rittel's Super Solvent to each gallon of water. Allow the skin to soak for 30 minutes then rinse. Allow the skin to drain for 10 to 20 minutes. Mix 1 part Rittel's Bird-Tan to 1 part cool water. Apply the Bird-Tan tanning solution to all the flesh areas using a paintbrush as an applicator. Cover the inside of the skin thoroughly, then fold the skin flesh-to-flesh and allow the solution to penetrate for three to four hours. If you haven't skinned out the wing tips, inject Bird-Tan into those areas with a hypodermic needle. Fluff or tumble the skin to dry it.

Larger skins such as ostrich can be tanned using the combination EZ-100 and vegetable tan method. The first step is to tan the skins in the EZ-100 tanning solution. For every 1 pound of drained skin weight mix 2 quarts of

Carefully peel the skin away from the carcass using a sharp knife as needed.

water, ½ ounce (4½ level teaspoons) of Rittel's EZ-100 and 3 ounces of noniodized salt.

Before placing the skins in the tanning solution, check the pH level; it should read 4.0. If the pH isn't at 4.0, raise by adding some sodium bicarbonate dissolved in water, or lower it by adding some Saftee-Acid. Be extremely careful in adjusting the pH—a very little can cause big fluctuations. After placing the skins in the tan, check the pH level two to three hours later. If it varies, readjust until it again reads 4.0. Additional adjusting of the pH is usually not necessary. Leave the skins in the tanning solution 16 to 18 hours. Rinse and drain for 30 minutes.

Now retan the skins in a vegetable tanning solution. For every pound of drained skin weight mix 2 quarts of water and 1.6 ounces of quebracho vegetable extract powder.

Use no salt in this second solution, only hot water, to dissolve the vegetable leather extract powder. Then allow the solution to cool before placing the skins in the tan. Start the pH level at 4.5 and allow the skins to soak for two days. When tanned, use a very small amount of Saf-tee-Acid to lower the pH level to 3.5 to fix the vegetable tan. Continue to soak the skins at this lower pH level for one hour more.

Remove the skins and neutralize the tanning solution with a solution of 1 ounce of sodium bicarbonate (baking soda) to each gallon of water. Allow the hides to neutralize for one hour. Then drain them for 20 minutes—no longer.

Any number of materials may be used to preserve the skin.

While the skins are draining, mix an oil and hot water solution of 1 part Rittel's ProPlus Oil to 2 parts hot tap water. Use a paintbrush and apply the mixture to the flesh side of the skin while the oil is still hot. After applying, leave the skins lying open and flat to absorb the oil, which should take three to four hours. After the initial take-up of the oil, hang or tack the skins out to dry. When the skins are almost dry, begin to work and pull the fibers until the skin is dry and soft.

For effectively tanning three to five full ostrich skins, Rittel's suggests a list of the ingredients and quantities necessary.

2 quarts Saftee-Acid
2 quarts Super Solvent
1 pint Washer
2 lbs. sodium bicarbonate
2 lbs. EZ-100 tan
5 lbs. quebracho extract
1 gallon ProPlus Oil
1 salinometer
1 roll of pH papers range 0.0 to 3.0
1 roll of pH papers, range 3.0 to 5.5

CHAPTER 13

Skinning and Preserving Reptiles

T he skins from snakes and reptiles such as alligators have traditionally been tanned or made into leather. Reptiles provide beautifully figured skins that can be used for any number of items including boot trim, belts, wallets and many others.

ALLIGATORS

Skinning

The first step is skinning. On small- to medium-sized gators the carcass is skinned in the open-skin, belly-up method, much the same as used for small game and deer. With big gators, some skinners leave the back plate on the gator because it's almost impossible to tan properly. In this method the skinning cuts are made on the back, cutting around the back plate and leaving the belly skin intact.

Alligator hides will rot very quickly, and it's important to salt the hide immediately after skinning. Use 1 pound of salt per pound of hide and work the salt well into all cracks and crevices. Make sure all edges are covered as well. Fold the hide flesh-to-flesh, then roll it up and place it on an inclined area to drain. After two days unroll, brush off the old salt, add new salt and roll back up. If the skin is to be kept some time before tanning, it should either be frozen or placed in a tightly secured plastic bag and then in a plastic tub with a tight lid. Make sure enough salt has been added to the hide to keep it preserved.

Tanning

When ready to tan, the first step is to soak the skin in a relaxing bath to soften. This may require from two to four days. When the skin is softened, it is placed in a lime bath. This bath should consist of 1 pint of caustic lime to each gallon of water needed to cover the hide. Allow the hide to sit in the lime solution for a week or two, or until the scales are loosened. Make sure the hide is totally immersed and occasionally stir the hide to ensure all areas receive the lime.

Once the scales have become loosened, they are scraped off with a fleshing knife over a beam in much the same manner as for dehairing other hides. Then turn the hide over and thoroughly flesh it to remove all fat, flesh and inner membrane. Wash the fleshed and scaled hide in several changes of clean water.

Mix a neutralizing bath of 1 quart of vinegar to each 3 gallons of water. Immerse the hide in the neutralizing bath and leave it for 24 hours, stirring occasionally. Remove the hide from the neutralizing bath, wash well and allow the hide to drain for an hour.

The next step is to soak the hide in a pickle or acid bath. Any number of pickle baths may be used. Saftee-Acid pickle is an excellent choice. For every pound of drained skin weight mix 2 quarts of water, ½ ounce of Saftee-Acid (4½ teaspoons) and 1 pound (½ cup) of non-iodized salt. The solution should test at a 1.1 to 1.5 pH. Allow the skins to pickle in this solution for three to five days, stirring the solution at least twice a day. After three to five days, the skins should be thoroughly pickled and can safely be left in the pickle for up to four weeks. The salt content of the solution should read 40 to 45 percent on a salinometer.

After at least three days, remove the skins, drain them for 30 minutes and then shave them clean, making sure to get all the fat out of any folds or pockets of the flesh. Then degrease the skins using Rittel's Super Solvent Degreaser, 4 ounces for each gallon of water needed to cover the hides. Allow the hides to soak in this solution for an hour. Then wash the skins using 1 ounce of Rittel's Washer to every gallon of water, or a dishwashing detergent such as Joy or Dawn. Rinse well and return the skins to the pickling solution. Allow the skins to soak for another 24 hours or more then remove, rinse and drain.

Neutralize the skins with a solution of 1 ounce of sodium bicarbonate to every gallon of water needed to cover the hides. The pH should be 4.5 or slightly higher. Allow to soak for an hour, then rinse the skins and allow them to drain for about 30 minutes.

Bruce Rittel of Rittel's Tanning Supplies suggests tanning gators in an EZ-100 and vegetable combination tan. The first step is to tan the skins in the EZ-100 tanning solution. For every pound of drained skin weight mix 2 quarts of water, ½ ounce (4½ level teaspoons) of Rittel's EZ-100 and 3 ounces of noniodized salt.

Before placing the skins in the tanning solution, check the pH level; it should read 4.0. If the pH isn't at 4.0, raise by adding some sodium bicarbonate dissolved in water, or lower by adding some Saftee-Acid. Be extremely careful in adjusting the pH; a very little can cause big fluctuations. After placing the skins in the tan, check the pH level two to three hours later. If it varies, readjust until it again reads 4.0. Additional adjusting of the pH is usually not necessary. Leave the skins in the tanning solution 16 to 18 hours. Rinse and drain for 30 minutes.

Now retan the skins in a vegetable tanning solution. For every pound of drained skin weight mix 2 quarts of water and 1.6 ounces of vegetable extract powder. "You can use quebracho, gambier or sumac extract in this formula interchangeably," explains Rittel. "But keep in mind that the color of the finished leather will depend on which extract you choose. I personally like quebracho. It's a typical brown leather color."

Use no salt in this second solution, only hot water to dissolve the vegetable leather extract powder, then allow the solution to cool before placing the skins in the tan. Start the pH level at 4.5 and allow the skins to soak for two days. When tanned, use a very small amount of Saftee-Acid to lower the pH level to 3.5 to fix the vegetable tan. Continue to soak the skins at this lower pH level for one hour more.

Remove the skins and neutralize the tanning solution with a solution of 1 ounce of sodium bicarbonate (baking soda) to each gallon of water. Allow the hides to neutralize for one hour. Then drain them for 20 minutes—no longer.

While the skins are draining, mix an oil and hot water solution of 1 part Rittel's ProPlus Oil to 2 parts hot tap water. Use a paintbrush and apply the mixture to the flesh side of the skin while the oil is still hot. After applying, leave the skins lying open and flat to absorb the oil, which should take three to four hours. After the initial take-up of the oil, hang or tack the skins out to dry. When the skins are almost dry, begin to work and pull the fibers until the skin is dry and soft.

SNAKE SKIN

The skins of snakes can be preserved or tanned in a number of ways, depending on whether the skins are to be used as "display" or for leather projects. Snake skins sometimes pose a bit of a tanning problem due to the fact the skins are shed periodically. The strength of the skin depends on the timing of shedding and when you tan the skin. It, however, isn't something you can control, as you probably won't know when the snake last shed.

My first tanning experiments with snake skins, almost 30 years ago, were pretty primitive. One dandy hatband

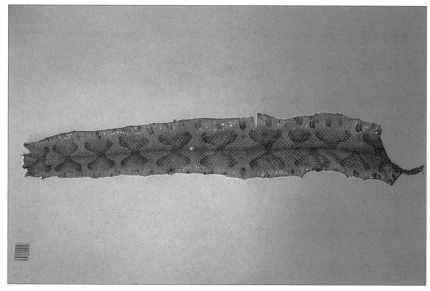

Snake skin provides a very attractive leather that can be used for a number of projects.

is now pretty well deteriorated. I used borax, salt, even automotive antifreeze, all at suggestions of others. I later used a salt-alum tan on the snake skin and it provided a longer-lived skin. Snake skins must first be pickled as with fur skins, using any of the pickle baths mentioned.

Skinning

The first step is proper skinning. Cut off the head and tack the tail to a work surface. Then use a sharp knife to slit the belly and peel the snake out of the skin. Game shears can also be used for this chore for cutting the belly. Once the snake is removed from the skin, use a very sharp knife to carefully flesh the flesh side of the skin. The edge of a tablespoon with one edge sharpened can also be used. Work from the tail toward the head. Be careful, as you can easily cut or tear the fragile skin at this point.

Fresh or frozen snake skins tan the best, but if you prefer to salt the skin to preserve it, then continue to tack the skin out flat on the work surface. A piece of plywood that can be moved around is a good choice. Apply salt liberally to the flesh side of the skin and rub it in well. Leave this layer of salt on the skin for two to three days, then brush it away and allow the skin to dry thoroughly. Place in a cool, dry area, safe from pets and critters. I had a house cat make a meal of one skin drying in such a manner. Do not expose the skin to heat or direct sunlight while it is

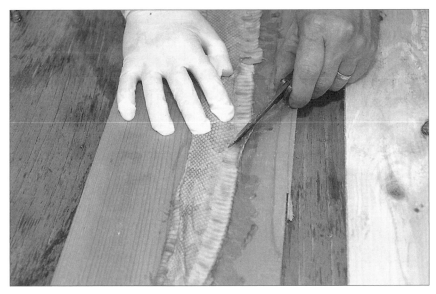

First step is to skin the snake and scrape the flesh side to remove all fat and membrane. For skins used for craft items, scrape off the scales.

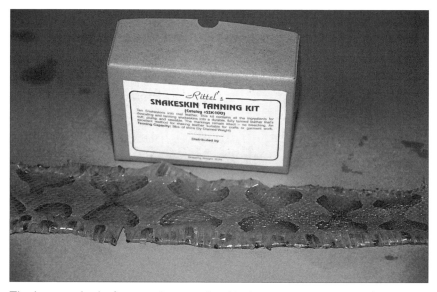

The best method of preserving a snake skin is to tan it using a regular tanning agent for snake skins. (Photo courtesy Rittel's Tanning Supplies).

drying. Heat can render snake skin stiff and untannable. Heat causes the fibers to gelatinize to a gluelike hardness, and these skins are almost impossible to relax and tan.

To freeze snake skins, place them in a plastic garbage bag and seal shut. Snakes normally shed their outer layer of skin to grow, and this may occur during the tanning process. If it does, remove the outer layer; this should not affect the skin.

Tanning

Producing a real leather from snake skin takes quite a bit more effort. Dried and frozen snake skins must first be placed in a relaxing or thawing bath before tanning. Use 2 pounds of salt to each gallon of water. Allow the skins to soak in this salt brine until they become soft and flexible. Then rinse and place in a pickle solution.

Freshly fleshed skins can be placed directly into a vinegar and salt pickling solution. The pickling solution is made by mixing 2 quarts of white vinegar with 2 quarts of water and adding 1 pound of salt. Mix enough solution to completely submerge the skins without crowding. The pH level should read 2.0 to 2.5. Allow the skins to soak in the pickle for two to three days. Actually the skins can be left in the pickle solution for several weeks. Stir the pickle at least once each day and don't expose it to temperatures below 50 degrees F.

When you are ready to tan the skins, remove them briefly from the pickle and rinse. Squeeze out the excess water and weigh the skins.

After the skins have been removed from the pickle solution, add to the pickling solution 6½ ounces by weight, or 5 fluid ounces by volume, or ⅔ cup of Rittel's Kwik-Tan per pound of snake skin weight. Stir the solution, and place the skins back in the solution. The pH level of the solution should read 4.0. If not, adjust as needed. Leave the skins in the tanning solution for 12 to 20 hours. Snake skins will fully tan within this time. When tanned, remove, rinse and drain for 20 to 30 minutes then apply the oil.

If using the snake skin for making craft items, the scales should be removed. For taxidermy or display purposes, the scales are usually left on the skin. Descale afer the skin is fully tanned. Rinse the skins in cold water,

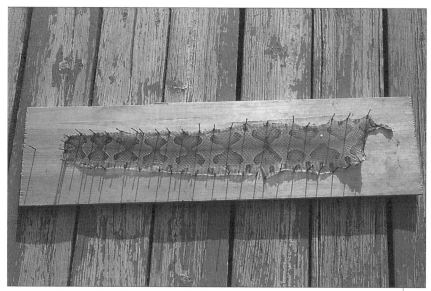

Snake skins for belts, hatbands and other projects are usually tacked out flat after tanning.

then crumple them up in your hands and you'll notice the scales beginning to fall away. Use a brass bristle brush to loosen any scales that stick. Continue the process until the skins are completely descaled.

Prepare an oiling mixture of 1 part ProPlus Oil to 2 parts hot tap water. Rub or brush the mixture onto the flesh side of the snake skin while the oil is still hot.

For taxidermy or display purposes, tack the skin out flat and allow the skin to soak up the oil for three to four hours. Then the skin can be mounted for taxidermy, or even frozen and mounted later. For the latter, use a roll of paper towels and put a layer on the flesh and then roll the skin up and freeze.

For display purposes, after oiling and drying, turn the skin over to display the makings, tack it down with decorative tacks and give it a coat of clear lacquer or a clear sealer to keep the scales from eventually curling.

For craft purposes, after the oiling process and when the skin is almost dry, work it gently with your hands to soften it and make it flexible. Then lightly sand the flesh side of the skin to a smooth suede finish.

Rittel's Snakeskin Tanning Kit contains all the necessary ingredients to produce real leather, except for the salt and vinegar, which can easily be purchased locally. Unlike other methods that use alum, alcohol or glycerine, Rittel's Snakeskin Tanning Kit produces a leather suitable for crafts and leatherwork. The leather retains the distinctive markings and plumps, and has excellent durability and strength.

FISH

Fish skins can also be tanned, and the skins of larger fish make attractive accessories and decorative ornaments. Some fish skins, such as shark, are traditionally tanned because of their unusual qualities. Fish skins are treated in the same basic methods as snake skins. They are normally well fleshed, salted, then stretched out to dry to preserve them.

Before tanning, the dried skins must be soaked in a relaxing bath to soften. Skins with scales must have the scales removed before the tanning process. For this step dissolve a pint of caustic lime in a gallon of water and immerse the skins in the solution. In a day or two the scales should come off fairly easily. Use a tablespoon as a scraper. Rinse in clear water, then place in a neutralizing solution of vinegar and water.

Fish skins can be tanned with any of the acid or acid-alum tans mentioned in chapter 3. Or use Rittel's Kwik-Tan.

Source List

Cabela's, 800–237–4444, www.cabelas.com

Dixie Gun Works, 800–238–6785, www.dixiegunworks.com

E Leather Supply, 877–433–8468, www.eleathersupply.com

Fiebing's Leather Finishes, The Leather Factory, 800–433–3201, www.leatherfactory.com

Funke Trap Tags & Supplies, 641–483–2597, www.funke-traptags.com

McKenzie Taxidermy Supply, 800–279–7985, www.mckenziesp.com

Minnesota Trapline Products, 320–599–4176, www.minn-trapprod.com

Nite Lite Company, 800–648–5483, www.HuntSmart.com

Rittel's Tanning Supplies, 508–822–3821, www.rittelsupplies.net

Tandy Leather, 888–890–1661, www.tandyleather.com

Van Dyke's, 800–843–3320, www.vandykestaxidermy.com

Index

A

Acid tanning materials, 8
Acid tans, 128
Adipose membrane, 7
Air drying
   large game hides, 122
   pelts, 106
   stretching frames or boards, 106
Alcohol turpentine formula, 55
Alligators
   skinning, 219–220
   tanning, 220–223
      drying and oiling, 223
      neutralizing, 220–221
      pickling, 221
      shaving, 221
      vegetable tanning solution, 222
Alum, 51, 137, 205. *See also* Salt-
      alum
   tanning, 51
   vegetable, 52
Alum-carbolic acid, 52
Aluminum sulphate, 51, 137
American bison
   hair on tanning
      for rugs and robes, 203
Ammonia, 167
Ammonia alum, 137
Ammonium aluminum sulphate, 51
Ancient tanning methods
   making buckskin, 176
Angle of weave, 7
Antelope
   buckskin, 175
   skinning, 83

Apron, 39
   for fleshing, 108
Author's fleshing beam, 22
Automotive antifreeze
   snake skin, 224

B

Back
   definition, 10
Backbone
   definition, 10
Badger
   skinning, 68, 70
Baking soda, 158
Bark tannage
   definition, 11
   domestic tanning, 200–202
      time allotted, 202
Bear skins, 96–99
   hair on tanning
      for rugs and robes, 203
   initial cuts, 98
Beavers
   degreased, 127
   drying
      skins, 24
   fleshing, 107
   open-pelt
      cuts for, 64
   skinned open method, 118
   skinning, 64, 76
      photos, 77–81
Belly
   definition, 10

Belly (*continued*)
  skinning, 80
    photos, 73–75
Bend
  definition, 10
Big game
  fleshing, 119
  modern methods of tanning hides,
      149–174
  skinning, 83–102
Birds, 211–217
  tanned and preserved skins, 211
Bird skins, 5
Bird-Tan, 60, 214
Bluish cast
  chrome tanning, 163
Bobcat
  skinning, 70
Bone scrapers, 175
Borax, 163
  to adjust the pH level, 164
  snake skin, 224
Brain matter
  for buckskin, 184–187
    forced into skin, 186
    tanned and smoked
        photo, 191
  for tanning, 48
Breaking bench, 32
  photo, 34
Breaking stakes, 30, 134, 142
  for buckskin, 188
  construction plan, 33
  photo, 34
  to soften skin, 143
Buckets and measuring cups
  importance of nonmetallic, 32
Buckskinning, 175
Buckskin-Tan, 60
Buckskin tanning, 23
  final step, 190
  making, 175–192

Buffalo
  buckskin, 175
  hair on tanning
      for rugs and robes, 203
  rawhide, 207
  skinning, 102
  tanned, 5
Bulls
  skinning, 100
  tanned, 5
Butchering and skinning area, 18
Butt
  definition, 10

C

Cabela's
  commercial tans
    hair or fur off tanning, 148
    Deer Hunter's Hide Tanning
        Formula, 57, 59, 170
    tanning fur-on skins, 140–146
Calf
  skinning, 100
Calf brains, 184
Calf liver, 184
Caping, 84, 94
  head for mounting
    skinning cuts needed, 95
  salting, 96
Carcass
  finished, 76
Caribou
  skinning, 83
Carpenter's vise, 29
Cased skinning, 63
  cuts for raccoon, 64
  illustrations, 78–81
Catechols, 50
Cattle
  hair on tanning

for rugs and robes, 203
  skinned hung head-down, 101
Caustic lime, 44
  fish tanning, 229
Chef's Choice
  sharpening knives, 39
Chemicals
  combination with vegetable tan
    fur-on skins, 139
  disposal, 61
  storage, 17
  for tanning, 43
Chemical tanning, 51–55
Chipper shredder, 39–40
Chrome-Tan, 60
Chrome tannage, 55–57, 128
  deer and big game, 160–165
    neutralizing, 164
    oil and finish, 163
    time allotted, 161–162
    washing, 163
  definition, 11
  domestic, 198
  mixture no. 1, 56
  mixture no. 2, 56
  technique, 8
Chronic wasting disease (CWD), 48,
    184
Citric acid, 159
Cleanup, 40
Clothes dryer, 40
Collagen, 6
Collagen from putrefying
  preservation, 9
Combination chemical and vegetable
    tan
  fur-on skins, 139
Combination tannage
  definition, 11
Combs, 39
Commercial acid tanning materials,
    8

Commercial oil-based tanning agents,
    170
Commercial tanning formulas, 58–60
Commercial tanning oils
  tanning fur-on skins, 140–146
Condensed tans, 50
Corium, 7
Cowhide, 4
  definition, 11
  skinning, 100
  tanned, 5
Coyote
  fleshing, 107
  Rittel's EZ-100, 139
  salt-alum, 137
  skinning, 70
  tanning method, 128
Crop
  definition, 10
Curved fleshing knife, 108

D

Deer
  fleshing, 119
  hides, 4
    modern methods of tanning,
      149–174
  skin
    fleshing beam, 18
  skinning, 83–102
  tanning, 149–174
Deer Hunter's Hide Tanning Formula
  process, 143–146
  tanning fur-on skins, 140–146
  time allotted, 143, 145
Degreased skins
  hang, 127
Degreaser
  sprinkling, 127
Degreasing, 14

Dehairing, 13, 20
  for buckskin, 177–183
  deer and big game, 151–154
  solution
    commercial, 42–44
    recipe, 42–44
Derma layers, 6
Domestic animals, 83–102
  skinned hung head-down, 101
  skinning, 99–102
Drained weight formula, 196
Draw knife, 108
Drying, 14, 103
  alligators, 223
  domestic hides, 197–198
  fur
    temperatures, 115–116
  hair and fur, 146
  pelt, 108
  pelts, 115–117
  putrefaction process, 9
  rawhide or beaver skins, 24
  snake skin, 228–229
  techniques, 114
Dry-rub tanning paste, 137
Dry salting, 5
Dry scraping, 177–178

E

Electric clothes dryer, 40
Elk
  buckskin, 175
  fleshing, 120
  rawhide, 207
  skinning, 83
Emu
  tanned, 211
Erector pili muscles, 7
Eye protection, 40

EZ-100 Rabbit Skin Tanning Method,
  130–134
EZ-100 tanning material, 59

F

Fat treating
  for buckskin, 187
Feet
  skinning, 72, 77–79, 82
Fiber bundles, 6
Finishing, 15
  deer and big game, 167–169
Fish skins
  tanning, 229–230
Fish-Tan, 60
Flank
  definition, 10
Fleshing, 12, 105–113
  after freezing, 105–107
  big game, 119
  for buckskin, 177–183
  deer, 119
  elk, 120
  moose, 120
  open-skinned pelts, 113
  rolled-up edge, 111
  tail, 112–113
  tools, 107–108
  white-tailed deer, 120
Fleshing beam, 18, 21, 28
  clean, 117
  drape hide over, 111
  illustrated, 22
  larger animals, 120
  photo, 29–31
  stand-up
    construction plans, 31
Fleshing knife, 36
  make your own, 38
  photo, 35

Flesh the hide, 6
Flint or bone scrapers, 37
Fluffing
  hair and fur, 146
Follicle, 8
Formic acid pickle, 163
Fox
  Rittel's EZ-100, 139
  skinning, 70
Freezing, 103
  deer and other big game hides,
    122–124
  small game skins, 119
Front feet. *See* Feet
Front legs. *See* Legs
Full grain
  definition, 11
Fur
  dried and fluffed, 145
Furbearers
  fleshing, 105–113
  preserving, 105
  skinning, 63–81
Fur-off tanning, 146–148
Fur-on tanning
  small game, 125–146
Fur pelts, 5
Furrier's combs and curry combs, 39
Fur-side in
  pelt drying, 108
Fur-side out
  pelt drying, 108
Fur stretchers, 24–26, 28
  photo, 25

G

Gambier, 51
Gambrels, 18, 19, 67, 85
  head-down, 83
  skinning deer, 83–84, 85

skinning domestic animals, 99,
    101
Game pole, hoists, and gambrels, 19
Gloves
  protective latex, 40
  rubber
    for fleshing, 108
Glutaraldehyde tanning, 57–58, 128
  deer and big game, 165–167
    time allotted, 165–167
  sheepskins, 198
Goats
  hides, 4, 5
  skinning, 83, 99–102, 100
Grain
  definition, 11
  layer, 6
Gray fox
  skinning, 70
Greasy skins, 127
  soaked before using TANNIT, 141
Grinder, 39–40
Groundhog
  skinning, 66

H

Hair
  scraping off, 152–153
Hair-off tanning
  deer and big game, 149–160
Hair-on heavy robe, 203–206
Hair-on hide
  tanning
    pickling, 205
    rinsing and drying, 206
    shaving, 204–205
Hair-on tanning
  deer and big game, 174
Heads
  to be mounted, 83–84

Heads (*continued*)
  skinning, 69, 82
    photo, 76
Heavy hides
  domestic tanning, 198–199
Heavy leather
  definition, 11
Hides
  damage, 1–3
  decay, 103
  definition, 3, 11
  domestic tanning, 198–199
  graded, 3
  for leather, 4
  preserved, 119
  preserving and storing, 103–124
  salting, 119
  soaking
    tubs and tanks, 26
  stiffness of
    continually check, 125
  stored dry or frozen, 119
Hide structure, 6
Hide terminology
  definitions, 10
Hoists, 18
  and gambrels, 19
Horses
  hair on tanning
    for rugs and robes, 203
  hides, 4
  skinning, 102
Hydrated builder's or caustic lime,
    44
Hypodermis, 7

I

Indian slickers, 33
Inside and small fleshing beam
  photo, 29, 30, 31

Inside tools, 28
Ivory Soap, 48

J

Junction layer, 7

K

Kip
  definition, 11
Kiwk-N-Eze, 60
Knives
  curved fleshing, 108
  draw, 108
  fleshing, 36
    make your own, 38
    photo, 35
  pelting, 36
  purchased fleshing, 37
  scudding, 33
  sharpening
    for fleshing, 108
  skinning, 33, 108
    photo, 35
Kwik-Tan, 60
  fish skins, 230

L

Large fleshing beam
  illustrated, 22
Large game
  skinned hung head-down, 101
Latigo, 209
Leather
  definition, 11

Legs
  front
    skinning, 87
  skinning, 77–79
Lime, 41
  hydrated builder's or caustic, 44
Liming, 13
  definition, 11
Long wooden stirring sticks, 33
Lutan F, 205
Lye, 43

M

Manufactured tanning formulas, 58
Marten
  skinning, 68, 70
Materials
  list of suppliers, 231
Mature cattle
  skinning, 100
Measuring devices
  importance of nonmetallic, 32
  photo, 34
Metal stretchers, 24–26, 114
Mink
  skinning, 68, 70
Moose
  fleshing, 120
  hair on tanning
    for rugs and robes, 203
  hides, 4
  skinning, 83
Mule hides, 4
Muskrat
  skinning, 70

N

Naphtha, 127

Naphtha soap
  for buckskin, 189
Neat's-foot oil, 48, 147, 167
  for buckskin, 188
Neck
  definition, 10
Neutralizing, 13
  bath
    for buckskin, 183
  bird skin tanning, 216
  deer and big game, 154
    chrome tanning, 164
    second time, 157
  formulas, 44
Nose
  skinning, 82

O

Oak bark
  tanning domestic hides, 200–202
Oak tannage
  definition, 11
Oil, 160
Oil-based tanning
  agents, 170
  solutions, 170–173
Oiling, 14, 48–49, 60
  alligators, 223
  chrome tanning
    deer and big game, 163
  deer and big game, 167–169
  and finishing, 60–61
  snake skin, 228–229
  tanning fur-on skins, 140–146
  temperature chart, 49
Open-pelt beaver, 64
Open-pelt rabbit, 64
Open-pelt raccoon
  cuts for, 64

Open-skinned pelt
  fleshed, 113
Open-skinned small game
  fleshing, 117
Open skinning, 63
Opossum
  skinning, 68, 70
Ostrich
  tanned, 211, 214
Otter
  skinning, 68, 70
Outside beam, 18
Outside skinning table, 18
Outside tools, 18–28
Outside workplace, 20
Oxalic acid, 54
  fur-off skins, 147–149
  immersion tan for small game,
      134–135
  time allotted, 135

P

Paper strips
  for testing pH, 32–33
Papillary
  definition, 11
Paste tanning mixture, 138
  time allotted, 138
Pelting knife, 36
Pelts
  air dry, 106
  finished, 76
  preserving and storing, 103–124
  stretched on wooden stretchers, 114
pH
  adjusting, 164
  and tanning agents, 195–196
  testing

  paper strips for, 32–33
Pickling, 13
  bath, 135
  deer and big game, 154–157
  formulas, 44–46
  neutralizing solution, 47
  solution, 42, 131, 133
Pickling solution
  salt and acid, 6, 42
Pigs
  skinning, 100
Plastic barrels, 26
Pliable, 14
  deer and big game, 167–169
  skin, 142
    methods, 171–172
Potash alum, 137
Potassium aluminum sulphate, 51
Power hone
  sharpening knives, 39
Predators
  fleshing, 105
  skinning, 63–81, 70–71
Preserving, 5–6, 9, 12
  bird skins, 231
  furs, 105–109
  hides, 103–124
  pelts, 103–124
  reptiles, 219–230
Products
  list of suppliers, 231
Protective latex gloves, 40
Protein, 6
Purchased fleshing knives, 37
Pyrogallol, 50

Q

Quebracho, 50, 173

R

Rabbits
  open-pelt, 64
  skinning, 65–66
  tanning method, 127–128
Raccoon
  cased-skin
    cuts for, 64
  degreased, 127
  fleshing, 107
  open-pelt
    cuts for, 64
  Rittel's EZ-100, 139
  salt-alum, 137
  skinning, 68–69
  tanning method, 128
Raw fur
  sold to buyers, 115
Rawhide, 207–209
  definition, 11
  drying, 24
Rear legs. *See* Feet; Legs
Red and gray fox
  skinning, 70
Relaxing bath, 132
  solution, 42
Reptiles, 5
  skinning and preserving, 219–230
Rinse, 14
Rittel, Bruce, 163
Rittel's Acid Bate
  softer hair, 205
Rittel's Bird-Tan, 214
Rittel's Ewe-Tan-It Sheepskin Tanning
    Kit, 193, 195
Rittel's EZ-100, 132
  commercial tans
    hair or fur off tanning, 148
  Rabbit Skin Tanning Method,
    130–134

Tanning Agent, 205
tanning solution
  deer and big game, 158
Rittel's Kwik-Tan
  fish skins, 230
Rittel's ProPlus Oil, 134, 160, 196–197
  bird skin tanning, 217
Rittel's Relaxer/Washer/Degreaser
  bird skin, 214
Rittel's Saftee-Acid, 46, 131
Rittel's Snakeskin Tanning Kit, 226,
    229
Rittel's Super Solvent, 205
Rittel's Tanning Supplies
  tanning chemicals, materials and
    tools, 59
Rittel's Trapline Tanning Kit, 139
Rolled-up edge
  fleshing, 111
Rubber gloves
  for fleshing, 108
Rug tanning, 203–206

S

Safe place for storage, 17
Safety, 40
  for fleshing, 108
  material disposal, 61
Saftee-Acid, 46, 53, 131
  bird skin tanning, 215
Salinometer, 32–33
Salt-alum
  coyote, 137
  formula, 52
  paste mixture
    bird skins, 231
  raccoon, 137
  tanning
    snake skin, 224

Salt-alum (*continued*)
  tanning method, 127–128
  tanning solution, 136–139
    time allotted, 137
Salt and acid
  pickling solution, 6, 42
  tanning fur-on hides, 135–136
  time allotted, 136
Salting, 103, 121
  cape, 96
  hides, 119
  skin, 5
  snake skin, 224
Scales
  photo, 34
Scrapers, 36
  bone, 175
  for buckskin, 181–183
  construction plan, 38
  flint or bone, 37
  photo, 37
  two hide
    authentic Native American
      artifacts, 36
Scraping
  dry, 177–178
  procedure, 8–9
Scraping off
  hair, 152–153
Scrub brushes, 39
Scudding, 14
Scudding knives, 33
Sebaceous glands, 7
Second neutralizing, 14
Second pickling, 14
Shank
  definition, 10
Shark skins, 5
Sharpening
  knives
    Chef's Choice, 39
    for fleshing, 108

power hone, 39
  photo, 35
  tools, 39
Shave
  definition, 11
Shaving, 14
Sheep
  skinning, 83, 99–102
Sheepskin, 5
  pickled, 6
Shoulder
  definition, 10
  skinning, 80
Shoulder stake, 24
Sides
  definition, 10, 11
Skin
  damage, 1–3
  defined, 3
  for furs, 3–4
  graded, 3
  layers
    illustrated, 7
  for leather, 4
  pliable, 142
    methods, 171–172
  structure, 6
  tanned into buckskin and
    leather, 4
Skinning
  beavers, 64, 71–76
  big game, 83–102
  birds, 211
  deer, 83–102
  definition, 12
  domestic animals, 99–102
  groundhog, 66
  methods, 63
    illustrated, 64
  muskrat, 70
  rabbits, 65–66
  raccoon, 68–69

reptiles, 219–230
small game, furbearers, and
    predators, 63–81
snake skin, 224–226
squirrels, 66
work area, 18
Skinning knives, 33, 108
    photo, 35
    with rounded point
        deer skinning, 89
Skinning pole, 18
Skinning table, 18
Skive
    definition, 11
Skunk
    skinning, 70
Slickers, 33
    illustrated, 35
Small fleshing beam, 28
Small game
    gambrels
        construction plan, 67
    skinning, 63–81, 65–67
    wall hangings or rugs, 126
Smoke curing
    for buckskin, 189–192
Smoking fire trench, 192
Snake skin, 223–229
    skinning, 224–226
    tanning, 226–229
        fleshing, 227
        oiling and drying, 228–229
        pickling, 227
Snakeskin Tanning Kit, 226, 229
Soaking, 12
    hides
        tubs and tanks, 26
Soap treating
    for buckskin, 187–189
Sodium acetate, 158
Softening, 14. See also Pliable
    deer and big game, 167–169

Softwood or hardwood ashes, 43
Sole leather, 209
Split leather
    definition, 12
Squirrels
    tanning method, 127–128
Stabilizing. See Preserving
Staking tool, 21
Stand-up fleshing beam
    construction plans, 31
Steers
    skinning, 100
Stiffness of hide
    continually check, 125
Stock salt, 122
Storing
    chemicals, 17
    dry or frozen
        hides, 119
    hides and pelts, 103–124
    methods, 103
    safe place, 17
Strap leather
    definition, 12
Stretchers, 20
    air dry, 106
    construction plan, 38
    fur, 24–26
        photo, 25
    illustrated, 23
    metal, 24–26, 114
    photo, 37
    wooden, 26
        advantage, 115
        make your own, 28
        pelts, 114
Stretching, 103, 113–115
Stretching frames, 20. See also
        Stretchers
    air dry, 106
    illustrated, 23
Sudoriferous glands, 7

Suede
  definition, 12
Sulphonic acid
  agent, 193
Sulphuric acid, 54
  paste formulas, 54–55
Sumac, 50
Supplies
  list of suppliers, 231
Sweat glands, 7
Syntan tanning agent, 59

T

Table
  outside skinning, 18
Tail
  completely split, 109
  definition, 10
  fleshing, 112–113
  skinning, 73, 81
  skin out, 69
  stripper, 69
Tandy Leather
  TANNIT, 55, 58, 170
    commercial tans
      hair or fur off tanning, 148
      penetration time varies, 142
      tanning fur-on skins, 140–146
      time allotted, 141
Tanks
  for soaking hides, 26
Tanner's frame, 24
  illustrated, 23
Tannin, 50
  definition, 12
Tanning, 1–15, 14
  alligators, 220–223
  basic materials, 47
  bird skins, 231–237
  chemicals, 43

deer and big game, 158–160
domestic hides and skins and hair-
    on robes, 193–206
formulas, 41–61
fur-on skins
    commercial tanning oils, 140–146
household chemicals, 47
importance of water, 17
materials, 41–61
methods
    small game and furbearers,
      127–128
oils, 128
    tanning fur-on skins, 140–146
small game and furbearers, 125–148
snake skin, 226–229
solutions
    made or purchased, 46
test for, 166
time allotted, 134
using brain, 48
Tanning agents
  rubbed into flesh side, 172
  sensitive to pH, 195–196
Tanning steps
  definitions, 12–15
Tanning terminology
  definitions, 11–12
TANNIT
  from Tandy Leather, 55, 58, 170
    commercial tans
      hair or fur off tanning, 148
      penetration time varies, 142
      tanning fur-on skins, 140–146
      time allotted, 141
Tawing, 135
Temperatures
  drying fur, 115–116
  oil tanning, 49
Tools, 17–40
  list of suppliers, 231
  outside, 18–28

Towels, 39
Traditional buckskin making, 177
Trophy heads
    to be mounted, 83–84
Tubs
    importance of nonmetallic, 32
    for soaking hides, 26
Turpentine and alcohol
    tanning method, 127–128
    tanning small game and furbearers,
        129–130
Two hide scrapers
    authentic Native American artifacts,
        36

U

Uncased or open-skinned pelt
    fleshed, 113

V

Vegetable bark tanning, 50
Vegetable extract tanning, 50
    domestic hides, 202–203
Vegetable tanning
    definition, 12
    solution
        alligators, 222
        bird skin tanning, 215
Ventilation
    working area, 17

W

Washing
    chrome tanning
        deer and big game, 163

Water
    and tanning, 17
    steps, 41
Waterproof
    skin, 190
Waterproof apron, 39
    for fleshing, 108
Water volume formula, 196
Weasel
    skinning, 70
Weighing
    hide, 155
White gas, 127
White-tailed deer
    fleshing, 120
    home tanning, 150
White vinegar, 159
White wood ashes, 178
Wolverine
    skinning, 68
Wood ashes, 42, 178
Wood choice
    fleshing beam, 18–19
Woodchuck
    rawhide, 207
Wooden slickers, 33
Wooden stirring sticks, 33
Wooden stretchers, 26
    advantage, 115
    for fur
        make your own, 28
Wool-on sheep skin
    tanning, 193–198
Workbench, 29
Workplace, 17–40
    importance of, 19
    outside, 20
    ventilation, 17
Wringer washing machine, 40